Photo by Gerry Goodstein

A scene from the Manhattan Theatre Club production of "Joined at the Head." Set design by James Noone.

# JOINED AT THE HEAD

## BY CATHERINE BUTTERFIELD

Revised Edition

★

DRAMATISTS
PLAY SERVICE
INC.

**SPECIAL NOTE**

Anyone receiving permission to produce JOINED AT THE HEAD is required to give credit to the Author as sole and exclusive Author of the Play on the title page of all programs distributed in connection with performances of the Play and in all instances in which the title of the Play appears for purposes of advertising, publicizing or otherwise exploiting the Play and/or a production thereof. The name of the Author must appear on a separate line, in which no other name appears, immediately beneath the title and in size of type equal to 50% of the size of the largest, most prominent letter used for the title of the Play. No person, firm or entity may receive credit larger or more prominent than that accorded the Author. The following acknowledgment must appear on the title page in all programs distributed in connection with performances of the Play:

Originally produced by the Manhattan Theatre Club on October 27, 1992.

**SPEACIAL NOTE ON ORIGINAL MUSIC**

The original music used in the Manhattan Theatre Club production may be obtained through the composer, Peter Moll, 170 Centre Street, Milton, MA 02186.

**SPECIAL NOTE ON SONGS AND RECORDINGS**

For performances of copyrighted songs, arrangements, or recordings mentioned in this Play, the permission of the copyright owner(s) must be obtained. Other songs, arrangements, or recordings may be substituted provided permission from the copyright owner(s) of such songs, arrangements or recordings is obtained; or songs, arrangements or recordings in the public domain may be substituted.

*For*
*Kathy and Peter*

JOINED AT THE HEAD was originally produced by Manhattan Theatre Club (Lynne Meadow, Artistic Director; Barry Grove, Managing Director) at City Center, in New York City, on October 27, 1992. It was directed by Pamela Berlin; the set design was by James Noone; the costume design was by Alvin B. Perry; the lighting design was by Natasha Katz; music was by Peter Moll; the sound design was by John Kilgore; and the production stage manager was Karen Moore. The cast was as follows:

MAGGIE MULRONEY ..............................................Ellen Parker
JIM BURROUGHS ............................................Kevin O'Rourke
MAGGY BURROUGHS ............................Catherine Butterfield
OTHERS ...................................................Neal Huff, Becca Lish,
Elizabeth Perry, John C. Vennema,
Sharon Washington and Michael Wells

# ACKNOWLEDGMENTS

My deep and heartfelt thanks to: Gilbert Parker and Lynne Meadow for making this possible, Larry Corsa for making my life beautiful, Chris Casady Borgers, Maggie Marshall and Melanie Webber for the support only a girlfriend can give, Ginny Butterfield for never giving up on her flaky daughter and most especially to the real life Maggy and Jim Burroughs, for sharing their lives with me and letting me see into places an outsider is usually never privy to. Their bravery and astounding good humor inspired the writing of this play and the living of my life.

# CHARACTERS

MAGGIE MULRONEY
JIM BURROUGHS
MAGGY BURROUGHS

## ENSEMBLE ROLES

ACTRESS #1 — 1st Political Woman, 1st Nurse, 2nd Woman at book signing (Christine), Mommy with baby carriage, Doctor, Arguing Woman (Optional: Make-up woman — segue into TV studio)

ACTRESS #2 — 2nd Political Woman, Muttering Woman, Visitor at hospital, 3rd Woman at book signing, Nora, Mrs. Mulroney, Older Woman

ACTRESS #3 — Engaged Woman, Coat Check Girl (Sandy), Woman in Wheelchair, 1st Woman at book signing (Kathy), 2nd Nurse, Younger Woman (Optional: Terwilliger assistant — segue into TV studio)

ACTOR #1 — 1st College Boy, Waiter #2, Waiter in restaurant (Bill), Orderly, Young Man at book signing, First Man (final Scene) (Optional: Lighting guy — segue into TV studio)

ACTOR #2 — 2nd College Boy, Waiter #1, Crystal Salesman, Visitor at hospital, Daddy with baby carriage, Second Man (final Scene) (Optional: Stage Manager — segue into TV studio)

ACTOR #3 — Engaged Man, Man in Pajamas, Raymond Terwilliger, Mr. Mulroney, Arguing Man

In the production at Manhattan Theatre Club, the Ensemble did all of the scene shifts as well, rolling pieces of furniture on and off as they were needed, handing over telephones, refilling wine glasses (transition from first to second Maggie/Jim dinner scene), etc. They were occasionally acknowledged by the three main characters, but were never intrusive to the playing of a scene.

# PLAYWRIGHT'S NOTES

In production, it is important that the action be kept as fluid as possible. For this reason, I recommend a minimalist set and simple set pieces. The Manhattan Theatre Club production used furniture on silent casters, which whisked in and out as the two Maggies spoke and set the scene in very little time.

As a playwright/actress, I am aware that there are certain actors' traps inherent in this script that I might as well mention now, to give you a running start on character. Following are a few suggestions which you should feel free to ignore, but I hope you won't.

1) In order for Maggie Mulroney's journey to be satisfying, I would like to encourage the actress playing her to dare to be a little tough, even unlikeable at times in Act One. This is a woman without friends who is learning how to become one. We should feel her initial resistance to the intimacy Jim and Maggy encourage, a resistance which can then break down in Act Two.

2) Maggy Burroughs is a full-blooded, no bullshit kind of a person. The temptations are to a) fall into the self-pity trap, and b) play her as a saint. Avoid both of them, please. Nothing is less attractive on stage than self-pity, and nobody believes a saint.

3) Although Jim's monologue in Act Two is his only chance to say what is really going on inside him, it is important that the actor playing him not regard this as an opportunity to pull out all the emotional stops. The more matter-of-fact this speech is delivered, the more powerful it will be. Please, no tears.

# JOINED AT THE HEAD

## ACT ONE

*Lights up on Maggie.*

MAGGIE. *(To the audience.)* I was walking down Newbury Street in Boston on a very brisk, very clear day, late afternoon. Low on the horizon, the white winter sun shone directly in my face. It dazzled me, this light. I could see shadow forms of people coming toward me, but I couldn't make out faces, and I couldn't make out buildings, and I felt like I was almost blind, although my eyes were wide open. How to describe it — I felt like a camera with its lens open too far. And you know, it's funny about the drivers in Boston, they don't honk very much. They drive like madmen, but they don't honk. Which is unexpected to a New Yorker, who expects not only honking but yelling, sirens, distant gunfire. So here I was, having this strange, silent walk down Newbury Street, strange not only because it seemed so civilized, but because, being blinded by this light, my sense of hearing was unusually keen. And without meaning to, I found myself eavesdropping on a number of conversations. *(Two College Boys appear. They speak without noticing Maggie.)*

1ST COLLEGE BOY. And then, you know, my mom asked her, "So tell me about yourself?" And she said, "Well, I was born and raised in California but I moved here to go to school." I mean, it sounded like *The Dating Game.* "I like tennis, skiing, and hope to become a dental hygienist." That kind of thing.

2ND COLLEGE BOY. Uh-huh. God, yeah.

1ST COLLEGE BOY. So everybody's passing the peas, and my Aunt Janice starts to talk about the trip she took to California,

9

and it looks like everything's gonna be okay, you know? *(Two Women walk by.)*

1ST POLITICAL WOMAN.  Oh, yeah, like we won this war. He got exactly what he wanted, he trashed the place, and he's still in power. That's an interesting definition of victory for our side.

2ND POLITICAL WOMAN.  The feel-good war of the nineties.

1ST COLLEGE BOY.  But then my dad turns to her and says, "So what do you kids do for excitement?" And she says, "Well, Jim and I are still in the early stages of our relationship, so basically we stay in bed and have sex all day."

2ND COLLEGE BOY.  She said that?

1ST COLLEGE BOY.  Yeah. She'll say anything. I think that's why I'm so crazy about her. Listen to this one.... *(Maggie comes up to a couple in their thirties, holding hands.)*

ENGAGED MAN.  Let me see it again. *(She holds up the ring on her finger.)*

ENGAGED WOMAN.  It's so beautiful. I can't believe how beautiful it is.

ENGAGED MAN.  I think we got the right one. I'm very proud of us.

ENGAGED WOMAN.  So am I. *(They kiss. A Woman walks by muttering to herself.)*

MUTTERING WOMAN.  Don't let it be what I think it is. For God's sake, don't let it be what I think it is. *(Two Men walk by.)*

WAITER #1.  I'm tired of that scrod joke. It wasn't funny ten years ago, and it's not funny now. Why can't they just order without making that stupid scrod joke?

WAITER #2.  What scrod joke?

WAITER #1.  Oh, please. You're a waiter in a seafood restaurant, and you've never heard the scrod joke?

ENGAGED WOMAN.  You were wonderful. When that guy started to pressure us, we just walked out.

ENGAGED MAN.  *(Overlapping.)* Actually, he wasn't pressuring us. He was just doing his job. I liked him.

ENGAGED WOMAN.  Well, if you thought he was so wonderful, why didn't you buy from him?

ENGAGED MAN.  I'm not saying he was wonderful. I was just

kind of enjoying him.

ENGAGED WOMAN. *(Pause.)* That's funny. I thought we were having the same experience, and now I find out we were having two different experiences.

ENGAGED MAN. We're having the same experience now, though, aren't we?

ENGAGED WOMAN. I don't know. Are we? *(They exit.)*

MAGGIE. That was it, really. Conversations. Fragments of conversations. Who knows where they were meant to lead? But I became so aware of how much life is going on all the time, how many stories, how many people are out there with their absolute reality that has nothing to do with my absolute reality. To them, I'm the backdrop. To me, they're mine. How often do we think of ourselves as backdrops for other peoples' lives? Not too often, I guess. We prefer to think of ourselves as being terribly significant. I remember being in New York once when a piece of scaffolding fell and bisected the head of a person a half a block ahead of me. I arrived in time to see the carnage, the hysteria. And I started thinking about the guy who'd been killed. An actor in his thirties, I read a few days later. The center of his own particular universe, until his universe was suddenly snatched away from him. All the rest of us, on that New York afternoon on 57th Street, were the backdrop for the particular drama that was his life. How strange it would have been for him to know ahead of time that the supporting cast was going to play the show out without him. A play with a vacuum where the leading man is supposed to be? Impossible! We all live with that illusion, don't we? And we all parade the streets daily, back and forth, oblivious to the fact that the next piece of scaffolding may be meant for us. And convinced that really, deep down in the truest part of life, we are nobody's backdrop. *(She moves to an area with a bed and a telephone.)* I was in my hotel room watching endless reruns of gratuitous slaughter in the Middle East when the phone rang. *(She picks up the phone.)* Hello? *(The lights come up on Jim Burroughs, a man of thirty-eight. He is slightly overweight, slightly graying, if he took care of himself he would be a good-looking man, but he hasn't been.)*

JIM. Maggie?

11

MAGGIE.  Yes.

JIM.  Maggie Mulroney?

MAGGIE.  Yes. Who's this?

JIM.  Brace yourself for a blast from the past. This is Jim Burroughs.

MAGGIE.  Jim! Oh, my God! I can't believe it. Where are you?

JIM.  I'm right here. In Boston.

MAGGIE.  Are you still living here?

JIM.  Sure am. Well, Norville, actually.

MAGGIE.  Oh, my God. You sound just the same! How did you get my number? How did you find out I was in town?

JIM.  I read it in the paper. "Maggie Mulroney will be signing copies of her new book at the Harvard Book Store Cafe" — You're famous, Maggie, girl.

MAGGIE.  I am not.

JIM.  Well, you're as close to famous as anybody I've ever known.

MAGGIE.  Jim, I can't believe we're talking to each other. I feel like we're still in high school.

JIM.  Well, give or take twenty years.

MAGGIE.  No.

JIM.  Twenty years.

MAGGIE.  That's impossible. What are you — I mean, how are you doing?

JIM.  I'm fine, just fine. Yourself?

MAGGIE.  I'm fine, too. *(A pause. They laugh.)* I'm sorry. I'm overwhelmed. I don't know what to say.

JIM.  Me, neither. Twenty years is a lot to catch up on. Would you like to get together and try this in person?

MAGGIE.  I'd love to. *(To audience.)* This, psychologically, is the moment in a conversation where you establish the boundaries of what is going to happen between a man and a woman. Naturally, both of us knew this instinctively.

JIM.  We can have dinner. Maybe you can come over to the house. I'd love you to meet my wife. *(Maggie looks knowingly at the audience.)*

MAGGIE.  That sounds wonderful. You have kids, too?

JIM.  No. No kids. We wanted to, but … oh look, we can talk

about everything over dinner. How about tomorrow night?

MAGGIE.  Great!

JIM.  I'll pick you up at five.

MAGGIE.  See you then. *(She hangs up.)* It was as easy as that. Twenty years of total silence, of not knowing, and rarely thinking about someone who was once a big reason you got up in the morning. And now, all at once, all of that is behind you. Suddenly, you're going to have a civilized dinner with him and his wife. Ain't life strange? *(Jim is standing next to two chairs L. Maggie approaches.)* He picked me up alone. *(Maggie walks toward the "car" and Jim, then walks right past him.)*

JIM.  Maggie!

MAGGIE.  *(Turning.)* Jim? Jim! *(She goes to him and they hug.)*

JIM.  You didn't recognize me.

MAGGIE.  No, I did, I do. It was the sun, it was in my eyes. *(To the audience.)* I didn't recognize him. He looked entirely different. I searched his face, trying to find the boy I'd known, but I couldn't find him. It was a little scary. *(They get into the "car.")* On the drive to his house I felt uneasy. Maybe this was a mistake. What could we possibly still have in common?

JIM.  You look great, Mag.

MAGGIE.  Thanks. You do, too.

JIM.  Success agrees with you.

MAGGIE.  Well, it's been a long haul. You should have met me a couple of years ago, you'd have said, "Poor Maggie. What a shame her life's not working out for her."

JIM.  Really? Sure looks like it's working out now. *(Pause.)* I'm taking us through Newbridge. Just for old time's sake.

MAGGIE.  Oh, good. It's been so long. Have things changed a lot?

JIM.  You'll be amazed.

MAGGIE.  At the changes?

JIM.  At how much is exactly the same. You recognize this road?

MAGGIE.  … No, not really. At least, I…. Oh!

JIM.  Remember now?

MAGGIE.  Yes.

JIM.  Our little detour.

MAGGIE.   It's still there?

JIM.   It sure is.

MAGGIE.   *(To audience.)* We used to pull over in his van and make love. We had a special spot. A tiny dirt road right ... wait, it's coming up. *(Maggie and Jim are both involved in the search.)* Right....

BOTH TOGETHER.   There! *(They laugh.)*

MAGGIE.   God, it's still there.

JIM.   It's still there. Remember how we used to lie in the van and watch the stars come out?

MAGGIE.   And then you'd drive me home at about eighty miles an hour on Lamarr Street. It was crazy. We took our life in our hands every night, and never gave it a second thought. We thought we were impervious.

JIM.   Completely invulnerable.

MAGGIE.   We're lucky we weren't killed.

JIM.   It never even crossed my mind at the time.

MAGGIE.   Me, neither. We were pretty wild, then, huh?

JIM.   Pretty wild. *(They smile at each other.)* I don't think I've ever felt as sure of myself since.

MAGGIE.   What do you do? I mean, for a living. Are you still a musician?

JIM.   No. I'm teaching. At the high school.

MAGGIE.   Really? Music?

JIM.   No. English. One of life's little ironies, wouldn't you say? Me, the one who couldn't wait to get out of town, teaching English to the next generation of fuck-ups at the high school. Somebody up there really has a twisted sense of humor.

MAGGIE.   Hey, but teaching, that's a wonderful thing to do. Not everybody can teach. I'll bet you're great at it.

JIM.   I am great at it. I even like it. That doesn't mean it's what I want to do for the rest of my life.

MAGGIE.   What do you want to do?

JIM.   Oh, hell. What don't I want to do? I want to swim the Ganges. I want to be a film director. I want to find a cure for cancer.

MAGGIE.   Noble aspirations.

JIM.   I want to be seventeen, and start all over again.

MAGGIE.  Really?

JIM.  *(Pause.)* No. No, I'm kidding about that.

MAGGIE.  *(To audience.)* But he had tears in his eyes. It was funny, this happened a number of times on the drive, but since the rest of him seemed so completely under control I started to think he had developed an eye condition. Men are an odd breed. Their emotions sneak out in the strangest ways.

JIM.  What do you want?

MAGGIE.  Me? At the moment, I want to write a very, very good book. I want it to come easily, and naturally, and I want the muse to be sitting on my shoulder the entire time.

JIM.  The whole time?

MAGGIE.  Not even a coffee break.

JIM.  What about marriage, children, that whole thing. Don't you want any of that?

MAGGIE.  How do you know I'm not married?

JIM.  I read an interview in the *Patriot Ledger.*

MAGGIE.  Oh. Well, it's not a big priority with me. I give it thought from time to time, but it's not all that high on my list.

JIM.  Uh-huh.

MAGGIE.  It's really not. I get so annoyed with these people who think that if you're not married your life is a total failure. Sometimes I think I could win the Nobel Prize, and some people would still think I was a failure because I wasn't married. I mean, big deal!

JIM.  Absolutely.

MAGGIE.  It's not necessarily the end of the world.

JIM.  Hey, it was just a question.

MAGGIE.  *(Pause.)* Right. Sorry. It's just, you know, a question I get asked a lot.

JIM.  Sure.

MAGGIE.  *(To audience.)* Okay, so I got a little defensive. Twenty years, and he still knew how to punch my buttons.

JIM.  I've been writing some myself. Music, I mean.

MAGGIE.  Really? I'd love to hear it sometime.

JIM.  It's not for general consumption. I mean, I'd never expect to market it or anything.

MAGGIE.  So what? I remember how talented you were, Jim.

JIM. *(Brightening.)* Yeah — you know I do think some of it's pretty good. I really do.

MAGGIE. *(To audience.)* There he was, the boy I knew! He was still there. I just hadn't noticed.

JIM. So far, the only person who's heard any of it is Maggy. And of course, what's she going to say? She loves me.

MAGGIE. Maggie?

JIM. Yeah. Didn't I mention that to you? My wife's name is Maggy, too.

MAGGIE. Really?

JIM. Yeah. Only she spells hers with a Y. Wild, huh? The two big loves of my life, with the same name.

MAGGIE. *(To audience.)* I hadn't known that. I mean about being one of two big loves.

JIM. You're going to love her. In some ways you're very much alike.

MAGGIE. You know, I always get a little nervous when people tell me I'll love someone because they're so much like me. Generally, I can't stand people who remind me of me.

JIM. I'm talking sense of humor, that kind of thing. In other ways you're very different. Do you remember Maggy McClintock?

MAGGIE. No.

JIM. You probably will when you see her. She was a cheer-leader.

MAGGIE. Jim. How could someone who was a cheerleader in high school be anything like me?

JIM. Basically, she did it just to spite everyone.

MAGGIE. Oh. That sounds like me.

JIM. As kind of an extended joke. She was a year behind us, I didn't know her then. I met her years later at a Fourth of July parade. We started making rude comments together about the floats, and realized we had causticity in common. It's a won-derful bond, being caustic together. Don't you find?

MAGGIE. I guess. *(To audience.)* My imagination was running wild. I was ready for some kind of cross between Christie Brink-ley and Dorothy Parker.

JIM. Well, here we are. *(They stand and walk toward the door of the house.)*

MAGGIE.  Wow. What a wonderful old house. How long have you lived here?

JIM.  Six years. Uh, by the way. There's one other thing you should know about Maggy. *(Maggy appears at the door. Her head is wrapped in a brightly colored scarf.)* She has cancer.

MAGGY.  Hi, Maggie! *(She hugs Maggie.)* Good to see you. Come on in. *(They enter the house. It is very New Englandy — old, wood floors, wood-burning stove.)* How was the drive out?

JIM.  Good. I showed her Newbridge, since she hadn't seen it in so long.

MAGGY.  Hasn't changed, has it?

MAGGIE.  No. It's kind of amazing. So much else has. I mean, in the rest of the world.

MAGGY.  Actually, we have, too. You just can't see it at first.

JIM.  *(To Maggie.)* Do you recognize Mag now?

MAGGIE.  Uh, well, I kind of hate to say this, but no. *(To Maggy.)* You seem to recognize me.

MAGGY.  Oh, sure. You haven't changed much. Would you like a glass of wine?

MAGGIE.  Sure. Great.

MAGGY.  *(Displaying a bottle of red wine.)* Jim bought this specially for the occasion.

JIM.  Let me get that, honey.

MAGGY.  No, no. I can get it. *(She works the cork off and pours.)*

MAGGIE..  You have a beautiful home. I love what you've done with it.

MAGGY.  Thanks. We got off to a good start on it, but lately it's had to take a back seat to other things. We hope to get back to it soon.

MAGGIE.  How old is this house?

JIM.  Over a hundred years.

MAGGIE.  Wow.

JIM.  Yeah. Lot of history. Lots of ghosts prowling around.

MAGGIE.  Seriously?

JIM.  If you believe in that stuff. Which I personally don't, but Maggy does.

MAGGY.  Sure, why not? I plan to prowl around when the time

comes, scare the shit out of everybody. Don't you?

JIM.  *(Slightly uncomfortable laugh.)* Well, here's to us.

MAGGIE and MAGGY.  To us.

MAGGY.  Jim says you're here to do some publicity on your new book.

MAGGIE.  Yeah. Book signings, that kind of thing.

MAGGY.  It sounds like it's already a big hit. I can see why. It's really funny.

MAGGIE.  You read it?

MAGGY.  Oh, sure. Jim did, too.

MAGGIE.  Wow, I'm flattered. How did you like it, Jim?

JIM.  Fine, fine. Very good. Was that supposed to be your dad?

MAGGIE.  Well, you know, with a few embellishments.

JIM.  Interesting.

MAGGIE.  Why?

JIM.  I remember him so differently.

MAGGIE.  Well, you know. It's fiction. Sometimes you have to distort reality to make things interesting.

JIM.  Sure.

MAGGIE.  And it's been so long since he died.

MAGGY.  He died? You didn't mention that in the book.

MAGGIE.  No. Too much of a downer. I wanted to keep it light.

MAGGY.  Oh. That's too bad, though. How did he die?

MAGGIE.  Uh, well, cancer, actually. *(There is a pause.)* So you were a cheerleader, huh? I'm trying to figure out why I don't remember you.

JIM.  I'll get the yearbook. Maybe that'll jog your memory. *(He exits up the stairs.)*

MAGGY.  I think you probably made more of an impression on me than I made on you. You were a pretty memorable figure at Newbridge High.

MAGGIE.  Really? I always thought of myself as kind of disenfranchised and out of it.

MAGGY.  No way. You were our resident angry young woman. I was completely in awe of you.

MAGGIE.  You were?

MAGGY.  Oh, yeah. I think a lot of us were. Do you remember a little thing called Moratorium Day?

MAGGIE.   Sure. The protest day. "Let's get our Dick out of Cambodia."

MAGGY.   I remember the day you were running around trying to drum up support for it. You came storming into the gym where we were practicing cheers and said, "Cut school tomorrow and come into Boston for Moratorium Day. Everybody who objects to this obscene war is doing it, even people like you." I liked that. Even people like us. Even hopelessly shallow rally girls were trooping into Boston for Moratorium Day.

MAGGIE.   Tact was never my strong suit.

MAGGY.   And remember Beth Folger? She said to you, "Do you realize what tomorrow is? It's the day before the game with Dover. We've got to practice." And you gave us a look of total disgust and said, "Why don't you girls stick your pom-poms up your pudenda?" Then you marched off.

MAGGIE.   *(Laughing.)* Really? I'm not even sure that's proper English.

MAGGY.   We got the point.

MAGGIE.   I was such a big mouth back then. I'm surprised somebody didn't pop me one.

MAGGY.   Oh no, I thought you were wonderful. I have to admit some of the other girls thought you were a bit of a crackpot. I mean, there you were fomenting revolution while the rest of us were setting our hair on orange juice cans. You kind of caught us by surprise.

MAGGIE.   I never fomented revolution. I remember having a cause or two, but I mean I never blew anything up

MAGGY.   Yeah. I think I was secretly a little disappointed about that.

MAGGIE.   Did you go to the protest?

MAGGY.   No. I had some family problems. Wish I could have, though. I'll bet it was inspiring.

MAGGIE.   Yeah. It was okay.

MAGGY.   Oh well, next life.

JIM.   *(Coming downstairs.)* Here it is. The chronicle of our innocence. Mag and I page through it now and then when we need a good laugh. Check out the inscriptions.

MAGGY.   *(Reading.)* Here's one from Pam Brogan — "To a beautiful person and talented human being. Don't ever forget to seek the light and live forever free." Ah, the sixties.

MAGGIE.   How could we have worn our hair this way? My mom always used to say, "Your hair looks like you're hanging curtains." I had no idea what she meant.

MAGGY.   I personally slaved for hours for that curtain effect.

MAGGIE.   Mine was a product of sheer neglect. "To Jim, thanks for putting up with me in chem class. You are a wonderful human being and I'm so glad I got the chance to know you. Best wishes forever, Gina Lazlo." God! Gina Lazlo! She took chemistry? I always thought of her as a certified idiot.

JIM.   A beautiful certified idiot, and if there was one thing Gina was definitely an expert in, it was chemistry.

MAGGY.   *(Laughing.)* Listen to him. My Don Juan.

MAGGIE.   Jim had a major crush on Gina Lazlo.

JIM.   I did not. I mean I thought she was sexy and everything, but so did everyone else. I didn't have the nerve to come on to Gina Lazlo.

MAGGIE.   Jim Burroughs, what are you talking about? What about the night of our senior prom?

JIM.   What about it?

MAGGIE.   You dumped me for her!

JIM.   What? I did not.

MAGGIE.   You most certainly did, too.

MAGGY.   Jim! You dumped her at the senior prom?

JIM.   No, I didn't … did I?

MAGGIE.   Yes! Why would I make a thing like that up?

JIM.   God…. I did, didn't I?

MAGGIE.   I had to hitch a ride home, it was completely humiliating.

MAGGY.   You hitchhiked? In your prom dress?

MAGGIE.   It was a night to remember.

JIM.   Yeah, but wait a minute. Then you broke my window, remember that? You went over to my house and broke my bedroom window with a rock.

MAGGIE.   I did not.

JIM.   You did, too!

MAGGIE.  Well, you deserved it.

MAGGY.  *(Laughing.)* This sounds like a really stable relationship you two had going.

MAGGIE.  Oh, we were hopeless.

MAGGY.  Well, I think it's time to bury the hatchet, don't you? I mean, it's been twenty years.

JIM.  Maggie, I humbly beg your pardon for dropping you at the senior prom.

MAGGIE.  *(Grudgingly.)* Okay. I forgive you. Sorry I broke your window.

JIM.  My dad made me pay for it.

MAGGY.  Jim!

JIM.  Okay, okay. I accept your apology.

MAGGIE.  Thanks. *(To audience.)* It was funny, I walked into this house and felt totally accepted. I wasn't a threat, there were no weird vibes. She seemed completely unfazed.

MAGGY.  Are you married, Maggie?

JIM.  Uh-oh. Look out.

MAGGIE.  No, no. Can't find a man who isn't threatened by me. *(Pause.)* That sounds kind of obnoxious. I just haven't met the right guy, I guess.

MAGGY.  I have a lot of girlfriends with the same problem. There's something funny going on between the sexes these days. Everybody's jockeying for position like a gun's going to go off any minute.

MAGGIE.  Yeah. Or, I don't know. Maybe it's me.

MAGGY.  Why would it be you?

MAGGIE.  Oh, I don't know....

MAGGY.  It's not you, Maggie. Don't worry about that.

JIM.  Hey, how come Maggy can ask that question and it's okay, but I ask it and I get my head bitten off? This isn't fair. *(The phone rings.)* That'll be the phone. Hello?... Uh, yes, she's right here. *(To Maggie.)* It's for you.

MAGGIE.  Oh, thanks. *(She grabs her bag and takes the phone.)* Hello?... Shoot. *(She takes a little notebook from her bag, scribbles in it.)* Uh-huh.... Okay.... Okay.... What time?... Okay. Thanks. *(Hanging up.)* Sorry, it was my service. Looks like I've got another interview coming up.

MAGGY.   How exciting!

MAGGIE.   It's not exciting at all, believe me. It's grueling. But you've gotta do it, it goes with the territory. It seems like someone else controls every move I make.

MAGGY.   How did they get this number?

MAGGIE.   I ... gave it to them. Ooops. *(They all laugh.)* Let's find a picture of Maggy, where are the cheerleader pictures?

MAGGY.   Jim, there's you.

MAGGIE.   I remember that picture. Jim Morrison lives.

JIM.   And Maggie, there's you.

MAGGIE.   Oh, yuch. I hate that shot. I look like Squeaky Fromme.

JIM.   *(Laughing.)* Squeaky Fromme!

MAGGIE.   Feel free to disagree with me.

JIM.   No, it's true. It's really true!

MAGGY.   Oh, it is not. She looks pretty.

JIM.   Okay, here we are, here we are. Here's my Maggy. With all her fellow leaders of the cheer.

MAGGIE.   Where?

JIM.   Right there. *(He points.)*

MAGGIE.   *(Light dawning.)* Oh! *(She looks up at Maggy.)* I remember you!

MAGGY.   Hi.

MAGGIE.   Hi. *(To audience.)* I did remember her. I never knew her, but I remembered her distinctly. She must have lived near the school — I took the bus, and I'd frequently see her walking as we passed. She always looked so put together: shiny hair that swung back and forth as she walked, usually some nice skirt and sweater that looked freshly cleaned and pressed. And yet an air of tension around her, as though she were walking in a perfectly constructed bubble. But tonight, the woman before me was nothing like my high school recollections. I looked at her and the same thought kept ringing in my head — this woman has cancer?

MAGGY.   Are you hungry, Maggie?

MAGGIE.   Yeah, I am.

MAGGY.   Jim, you?

JIM.   Starved.

MAGGY.   Then let's go.

MAGGIE.   *(To audience.)* We went to an Italian restaurant. *(They sit at a table. A Waiter brings them drinks.)* It was a wonderful evening. We laughed more than I'd laughed in ages. Jim was in particularly fine form. He told story after story about people and places I thought I'd long forgotten. The food was sensational, and although Maggy ate very little she kept encouraging us to eat.

JIM.   ... and I was so upset that Ken Diamond got the Harvard Book Award instead of me, that when they told me I got the Brown Book Award, I was like, "Yeah, so what?" And you know, then I ended up going to B.U. and everything. And it wasn't until 1981 when I was typing up a resume that I said to myself, "Idiot! Why didn't you apply to Brown?"

MAGGIE.   Maybe you just thought they were giving you a brown book?

JIM.   *(Laughing.)* Yeah, that was it. "Ladies and gentlemen, we'd like to present Ken Diamond with the Harvard Book Award, and for Jim Burroughs we have this lovely brown book."

MAGGY.   *(Laughing.)* As a consolation prize.

MAGGIE.   Nothing written in it, but it is this lovely shade of brown. *(They are laughing convulsively by now. The Waiter walks by and looks slightly concerned.)*

JIM.   Oh, God. Is this really funny, or is there something wrong with us?

MAGGIE.   I think this is what is called making a scene.

MAGGY.   Oh, good. I've always wanted to make a scene. I'm waiting for the maitre d' to come over and say, "Excuse me, but we couldn't help noticing that you three are making a scene."

JIM.   "Perhaps you didn't notice the sign as you came in — absolutely no t-shirts, dogs or scene making in the restaurant."

MAGGY.   And I'll say, "Please sir, take pity on a poor girl. I'm going in for chemo at nine in the morning, and this may be my last chance to make a really good scene."

JIM.   "Avaunt!" he'll say. "Down with the sign! Let the scene making begin."

MAGGY.   Avaunt? Do you really think he'll say, "Avaunt!"

JIM.   He's a Shakespearean actor on the side.

23

MAGGIE.   Um, so you're going to the hospital tomorrow?

MAGGY.   Yeah. Chemotherapy.

MAGGIE.   Are you ... how do you feel about that?

JIM.   Well, she'd rather be on the beach at Maui, but that wasn't one of the options.

MAGGIE.   I'm sorry, that was a kind of a tactless —

MAGGY.   No, that's a fair question.

MAGGIE.   I've just never really understood ... I mean, what's it like?

MAGGY.   First you feel like shit, then you feel better, then you feel like *total* shit, and then hopefully after that you feel much better. Somewhere along the way your hair falls out. It's a process.

JIM.   What they do is, they bring you as close to the edge as they can without actually killing you. Then they count on the natural strength of your body to kick in and build things up again.

MAGGY.   Fortunately, I have a pretty strong constitution. In fact, aside from the fact that I have cancer, I'm in incredibly good health. But that's kind of like, "Aside from that, Mrs. Lincoln ..."

JIM.   The last one made her feel much better for quite some time. In fact, we thought we had it on the run. But it's deceptive.

MAGGY.   We're kind of on the retreat right now. We're trying to gain back a little ground, but then even when you get it, it's like Kuwait. The enemy has gone in and trashed it so bad, you're not even sure it's worth having.

JIM.   It's worth having.

MAGGY.   Yeah. Yeah, it's worth having. I'm kidding. *(There is a pause. Some music plays softly in the background.)*

JIM.   Hey, Mag, listen. They're playing our song.

MAGGY.   Playing our song? That's elevator music.

JIM.   Oh, yeah? Listen.

MAGGY.   *(Pause.)* Oh, my God. "Whiter Shade of Pale?"*

MAGGIE.   Muzak Procol Harum. Now I've heard everything.

JIM.   *(Getting up.)* Dance with me, baby. We can't let this op-

* See Special Note on Songs and Recordings on copyright page.

portunity go by.

MAGGY.   Dance with you? Here? Are you crazy?

JIM.   Not at all. You said you always wanted to make a really good scene.

MAGGY.   That's true, I did, didn't I?

JIM.   Your wish is my command. *(He whisks her into his arms and they begin to dance, laughingly at first, then she puts her head on his shoulder and they move more slowly. Maggie watches them.*

MAGGIE.   *(To audience.)* They were so in love. It was almost painful to watch. Maggy seemed so calm and serene, she didn't look ill in any way. Only later did I find out about all the pills she popped just to be able to be with us that night. Jim looked like a man who had just met the most beautiful woman in the world and couldn't believe his good fortune that she had agreed to dance with him. I watched them in awe. I'd never seen anything quite like it. It was as though they were the only two people in the whole restaurant. The only two people in the universe. *(The music stops.)*

JIM.   Maggy Burroughs, you have just made a scene.

MAGGY.   Thank you, my love. Another life-long wish come true. *(They kiss and go back to the table.)* Maggie, are you feeling totally abandoned?

MAGGIE.   No, just jealous. I want to make a really good scene.

MAGGY.   Shall we all three dance the next dance?

MAGGIE.   Maybe we should organize the other diners and form a conga line.

MAGGY.   Yes! A conga line. What's playing? *(They listen. The next song has no beat whatsoever.)*

JIM.   Good luck, girls.

MAGGIE.   Oh, well.

MAGGY.   Maybe we should have a seriously dangerous dessert instead.

JIM.   Ah, an inspired idea. Garçon! *(The Waiter approaches.)* Do you hate being called Garçon?

WAITER.   Are you planning to tip well?

JIM.   Possibly.

WAITER.   Then you can call me anything you want.

JIM.   Excellent! Well, Heathcliff, we are thinking of going out on a limb and ordering dessert. What do you think about that?

WAITER.  Very exciting.

JIM.  Do you have dessert menus?

WAITER.  Yes, we do. *(Pause.)* Would you like to see them?

JIM.  Heathcliff, old man, we'd love to see them. *(The Waiter hands them the menus under his arm.)*

MAGGIE.  We looked at our menus. I don't know why, but I was feeling very happy. It was as if we were the Three Musketeers, all for one and one for all. I lowered my menu to speak, when suddenly I saw a look pass between the two of them. A look that was so emotionally charged it almost knocked me off my chair. It spoke of a deep love, the kind that can only spring from pain. But there was more. In his eyes I could see everything from fear to desperation to a kind of plea — "Don't leave me!" Her look to him was much more simple. "Courage," it said. In that moment, I realized why Maggy was not threatened by me. These two had something between them that went beyond emotions like jealousy. When you're dealing with something as earth shaking as death, jealousy is an emotion that just ceases to have meaning. *(Maggy closes her menu and addresses the audience for the first time.)*

MAGGY.  Excuse me, I hate to interrupt, but I've got to say something here. This woman is romanticizing. Now, I can understand why she's doing it, I mean she's a writer, I've read her stuff and I can tell her heart's in the right place. But this is my life here, and she's turning it into some kind of Gothic novel. *(To Maggie.)* Please. I don't mean to ruin your little whatever-this-thing-is, but there's a certain amount of bullshit going on, and I'd like to take the opportunity to set the record straight. You don't mind, do you?

MAGGIE.  *(Horrified.)* What are you doing?

MAGGY.  I just thought I'd correct a few misconceptions. Okay with you?

MAGGIE.  No. I'm sorry, but it is not okay with me. Please sit down. *(Maggy remains standing.)* Maggy, come on. Okay, I'll admit I've allowed myself a little artistic license. But all writers do that. Now, maybe I haven't gotten all the facts completely straight, but since this is fiction —

MAGGY.   This is not fiction. This is my life you're serving up before everyone, and I think I have the right to put in my two cents worth.

MAGGIE.   Well, could you maybe do it after I've told the whole story?

MAGGY.   No. Sorry. I thought I could at first, but that last monologue of yours was so over the top I just had to say something. Listen, I don't mean to rain on your parade. But I should think in the interests of accuracy, you'd like to hear what I have to say.

MAGGIE.   *(Wounded.)* Fine. Go ahead.

MAGGY.   I've hurt your feelings?

MAGGIE.   No, no. Say what you have to say.

MAGGY.   Okay, well —

MAGGIE.   But I'd just like to add that this story is meant to be a tribute to you. I am working very hard to present your story in a light that will be an inspiration for others, and perhaps even immortalize you.

MAGGY.   Immortalize me? Boy, are you barking up the wrong tree. I'm just one other person who got cancer. No more or less mortal than anybody else.

MAGGIE.   Okay, perhaps that's true. But don't you see that the very act of making your life into a story suddenly gives it dramatic proportions? It invests it with a meaning that it might not have otherwise had.

MAGGY.   Excuse me. Are you trying to tell me that my life didn't have meaning?

MAGGIE.   No! Not at all.

MAGGY.   Okay, good. Then since we both agree that my life had meaning regardless of whether you chose to put it down on a piece of paper or not, I think I should be able to address a few points here. *(To audience.)* Don't you?

MAGGIE.   Okay, okay.

MAGGY.   You give me leave to speak?

MAGGIE.   Speak, speak.

MAGGY.   Thank you. *(To audience.)* Okay, first of all, let me just say that Maggie was right about one thing. I did like her. I still do. I had the same feeling she did when we met, that we were maybe sisters in another life, or brothers. Dragged slabs of stone up the same pyramid, whatever. And having the same name and all, that kind of heightened the effect. We ran with different crowds in high school: hers was the angry politicos, the early freaks and dope smokers that we all looked down upon. Mine was the party crowd. The funny thing is, I realize now I was really hanging out with the wrong people. I would have been a lot happier with all the angry ones, and I would probably be a lot healthier today if I'd started blowing off steam at an early age. But that's another story.

MAGGIE.    Please don't tell it now.

MAGGY.    Don't worry, I won't. Now, about this Three Musketeers thing....

MAGGIE.    It was just an allusion. I didn't mean to suggest that we —

MAGGY.    Yeah, okay, but it's still over the top. I mean for God's sake, I'd only just met you that night. Jim hadn't seen you in twenty years. How could you suddenly see us as an inseparable threesome?

MAGGIE.    It was the way I was feeling! I didn't say it was the way you were feeling. I don't have that many close friends in my life, and that evening was very important to me —

MAGGY.    Why don't you have any close friends?

MAGGIE.    I didn't say I don't have any. It's just that with my lifestyle, and the lifestyle of my friends, — wait a minute, this is not where I want to go with this. This is your life we're examining here.

MAGGY.    Why can't we do a little looking at yours while we're at it?

MAGGIE.    Because that is not the intention of this piece! Now please, Maggy. I don't mind you putting in a few words, but let's not take this in an entirely different direction.

MAGGY.    Okay, okay. Sorry. *(Pause.)* But I think you might want to look into that no friends thing some time in the future.

MAGGIE.    Thank you. I will. Now, did you have anything more you wanted to add before I go on?

MAGGY.    Yes. That look. The meaning of that look.

MAGGIE.    That look was a devastating thing.

MAGGY. Yeah, okay, to you, maybe. To us, it was one of a thousand looks we'd given each other since this whole thing began. And listen, it's not fair to paint Jim as the wimpy one and me as some kind of saint. You didn't get to see the days when I was a whiney baby, or a total bitch and Jim was still solid as a rock. It's important you get that in, Mag. I want Jim to get his due.

MAGGIE. Okay.

MAGGY. And one more thing —

MAGGIE. Oh, come on, this isn't fair —

MAGGY. One more thing. I *was* jealous of you.

MAGGIE. You were?

MAGGY. Yes. But not for the reason you think. I was jealous because you were healthy, because you had your whole life ahead of you. I started wishing Jim had married you, so he wouldn't have to go through this shit with me.

MAGGIE. No.

MAGGY. Yes! Of course, yes. Do you have any idea of the guilt that a sick person carries around, knowing that they're ruining the lives of everyone they love? The whole experience is one big fucking drag, but the guilt thing is definitely a stand-out. *(Pause.)* Okay. I'm done. Carry on. *(She reopens her menu.)*

MAGGIE. *(Pause.)* Carry on? Carry on? You've just ruined my whole story here. How do you expect me to just "carry on"?

MAGGY. Well, come on. I mean, what was the original impulse behind this story?

MAGGIE. ... I don't know.

MAGGY. Yes, you do. You're just sulking.

MAGGIE. Well I think I have the right to sulk! I don't even dare say anything more about you, I'm afraid you're going to stand up and say it's bullshit again.

MAGGY. No. I won't. I promise.

MAGGIE. You know, you've taken the heroic aspect right out of this thing.

MAGGY. How? By telling the truth?

MAGGIE. By emphasizing aspects of your character that we don't need to know.

MAGGY. Sorry. This is me. Take it or leave it. Look, I promise,

I won't say another word. I just wanted to start you off on the right foot. Now that I've got you going, things should go much more smoothly. By the way, I loved the opening. All those people walking around talking. Neat stuff. I don't know what it meant, but it looked cool.

MAGGIE.  Thanks. *(To audience.)* Sorry about that. I know how irritating it is to have the flow interrupted. I didn't mean this to be a Brechtian evening, I was hoping you'd be able to indulge your emotions from time to time. So feel free, in the future, to — OH, THIS IS HORRIBLE!

MAGGY.  No, no. You can do it. Come on, I'm on your side. *(Maggie takes a deep breath, shakes out her arms.)* Good, that's good. Get relaxed, shake it out, good idea. Okay — *(A cheerleader.)* Let's go!

MAGGIE.  *(To audience. Reluctantly, at first.)* Well, like I said, I found that look that passed between them incredibly moving. Whatever it meant. *(She looks to Maggy, who remains immobile.)* And I also felt very much on the outside of their experience, very alone for a minute. But as has been already said, why wouldn't I feel alone? I hardly knew them. We finished dinner, and Jim went to get the car. *(They get up from the table. Maggy and Maggie walk over to a counter, behind which stands a Coat Check Girl.)*

COAT CHECK GIRL.  *(Handing them their coats.)* How was dinner, Mrs. Burroughs?

MAGGY.  Wonderful, Sandy. Hey, I thought you'd be in Europe by now.

COAT CHECK GIRL.  Three more days. I'm so excited. I've always wanted to see Europe.

MAGGY.  Me, too. Especially Italy.

COAT CHECK GIRL.  Oooh, Italy. You've never been to Europe?

MAGGY.  Not yet. Some day. *(Tipping her.)* Thanks, Sandy. Have a great time.

COAT CHECK GIRL.  I will! I might never come back. I might go out there and change my whole life!

MAGGIE.  Change her whole life. You think she will?

MAGGY.  Who knows? Anything is possible. We could open up

the papers some day and discover she's become … what?

MAGGIE.   Princess Sandy of Lichtenstein?

MAGGY.   Sure, why not? *(They laugh.)* This has been good for us, getting out like this.

MAGGIE.   Me, too.

MAGGY.   I haven't seen Jim this happy in ages. He was really excited when he heard you were in town. You should have seen the detective work he did to find out where you were staying.

MAGGIE.   Really?

MAGGY.   Yeah. He really wanted us to meet each other.

MAGGIE.   I can't believe we didn't know each other in high school. I get the feeling we would have been great friends, don't you?

MAGGY.   Nah. You would have hated me. I was such a goody-two-shoes back then, it was nauseating. Anyway, your friends all had me intimidated, they were so smart and disdainful of everything. Do you ever hear from Barb Mayer?

MAGGIE.   No.

MAGGY.   Or how about Susie Loman, or April Souther? You guys were all so tight.

MAGGIE.   No, we don't keep up. Different lives.

MAGGY.   Oh. *(Pause.)* Well, you're a big shot now, you've probably got a whole new slew of friends.

MAGGIE.   Yeah, I guess. Sometimes I wonder if they'd still be there if I weren't a success, though. It's hard to pick out your real friends sometimes, do you ever have that problem?

MAGGY.   Uh, no. At this point in my life, one thing that's really clear is who my friends are. *(She laughs.)* Listen, before Jim gets here, I just want to thank you for something.

MAGGIE.   What?

MAGGY.   For being my inspiration during a big moment in my life.

MAGGIE.   What big moment?

MAGGY.   Here comes Jim. I'd rather not talk about it in front of him. Just suffice it to say I'm in your debt, and thanks.

MAGGIE.   For what? Hey, you can't just leave it like this. I want to hear the story.

MAGGY.   You do? Well, hey, I'll be at Mass General for the next

31

few days, and I can have visitors. Maybe you could drop in.

MAGGIE.  Mass General?

MAGGY.  Yeah. You know where that is?

MAGGIE.  Uh, yeah. Yeah, I do. *(Pause.)*

MAGGY.  *(Seeing her discomfort.)* No, that's a stupid idea.

MAGGIE.  No....

MAGGY.  Yes, it is. You don't want to hang around a bunch of sick people.

MAGGIE.  It's not that. I just, you know, they keep me pretty busy, and —

MAGGY.  Sure. Well, listen, some other time. I'll be out before you know it, we have plenty of time. *(She exits.)*

MAGGIE.  *(To audience.)* Jim dropped Maggy off and drove me back to the hotel. *(Jim appears. He and Maggie get back into the car.)* She's fantastic, Jim.

JIM.  I thought you might enjoy each other.

MAGGIE.  You two are good together.

JIM.  Yeah. We do okay. *(Pause.)* She's a nurse, you know.

MAGGIE.  No, I didn't know.

JIM.  She works with children. She's taking a few months off right now, which is hard for her because she loves her work. But it'll work out fine. She'll have this chemo, we'll buy ourselves a little more time, and get back to life as usual.

MAGGIE.  Good. That'll be good.

JIM.  Yeah. That'll be good. *(There is a silence. We can hear the engine of the car. The street lights play on their faces intermittently.)*

MAGGIE.  Lamarr Street.

JIM.  Yeah. *(There is another pause. Then, as if by mutual consent, Jim speeds up the car. We hear the engine being pushed further and further. The street lights accelerate as they play over their faces. Neither says a word for about thirty terrifying seconds. Finally, Jim slows the car down, pulls over and parks. There is a pause. Then he puts his head on the steering wheel and begins to weep. He sobs audibly, and Maggie puts her arms around him. After a moment, he stops. They look at one another. It appears for a moment as though they might kiss, but they disengage. He starts up the car again. They drive in silence.)* What's that stuff you use on your hair?

MAGGIE.  Creme rinse. I've used it for ages.

JIM. Yeah. I remember. *(Pause.)* Maggy uses this herbal stuff. It smells really fresh. *(He drives a bit more, then pulls over.)* Well, here we are.

MAGGIE. *(Getting out.)* Will you call me? I want to hear how Maggy's chemo goes.

JIM. Sure. Or why don't you call me? I get kind of forgetful sometimes with all this going on.

MAGGIE. Oh, sure. *(She reaches out, puts a hand on his.)* It's going to be okay, Jim.

JIM. *(He pulls his hand away a little self-consciously, smiles.)* Oh, sure, yeah, I know. This is just a trying time. You look great, Mag, you really do. *(The engine starts, he waves.)* 'Bye! *(The lights go down on Jim.)*

MAGGIE. The next day I took a walk down Newbury Street. *(She walks over to a counter behind which stands a Salesman.)*

SALESMAN. Hi, can I help you?

MAGGIE. Well, I'm kind of interested in this crystal thing. I've heard a little bit about it, and I was thinking of maybe getting something for a friend. Although, *(She half turns.)* I don't know. Maybe this is silly.

SALESMAN. Not at all. What kind of stone were you thinking of getting?

MAGGIE. Well, I don't know. She's not very well, and —

SALESMAN. How about amethyst? It will put her spirit in balance and promote tranquillity.

MAGGIE. What? How could it do that? It's a stone.

SALESMAN. For thousands of years, stones have been recognized for their healing powers.

MAGGIE. By whom?

SALESMAN. By those who know.

MAGGIE. Scientists? Geologists?

SALESMAN. Not everything that happens in this world can be embraced by the parameters of science.

MAGGIE. Oh, I see. Voodoo men. Witch doctors.

SALESMAN. Are you sure you're interested in purchasing a crystal? You don't seem, frankly, like the optimum candidate.

MAGGIE. I'm not the candidate. I told you, it's for a friend.

SALESMAN. And what makes you think your friend might be

a candidate?

MAGGIE.  ... I don't know.

SALESMAN.  How about a Sugilite?

MAGGIE.  A what?

SALESMAN.  A Sugilite. They've only been mining it for the past forty years, but already it's renowned for its intense healing powers.

MAGGIE.  What does it look like? *(The Salesman takes a Sugilite out of the case.)* Not very pretty.

SALESMAN.  Beauty has nothing to do with a mineral's intrinsic power.

MAGGIE.  Oh. Sorry.

SALESMAN.  Have her — your friend is a woman?

MAGGIE.  Yes.

SALESMAN.  Have her put this by her bed, or even under her pillow.

MAGGIE.  Under her pillow! We're trying to cure her, not kill her.

SALESMAN.  Next to her bed then. And if the effects seem too powerful, tell her to move it farther away.

MAGGIE.  This is ridiculous. It's a rock!

SALESMAN.  Yes. I think we've already established that.

MAGGIE.  I'm not going to give a woman dying of cancer a rock to put under her pillow.

SALESMAN.  You know, you're the one who walked in here. I don't remember anyone dragging you through the door.

MAGGIE.  Okay, okay! I'll take it. Give me a big one. *(The scene changes to Mass General Hospital. A Nurse sits at a reception desk. An Orderly wheels a Young Woman by in a wheelchair. Maggie enters. She is visibly uneasy. She approaches the Nurses' stand.)* Hi.

NURSE.  Hi.

MAGGIE.  Um, is this where I can find Maggy Burroughs?

NURSE.  Maggy Burroughs, yes, she checked in about an hour ago.

MAGGIE.  Great. *(A Man in Pajamas walks down the hall pulling his IV along behind him. He looks scarily ill. He sees Maggie.)*

MAN IN PAJAMAS.  *(His face suddenly radiant with joy.)* Diane, you came! I was afraid you —

MAGGIE. *(Turning.)* Excuse me?

MAN IN PAJAMAS. Oh, I'm so sorry. I thought you were ... someone I know. My apologies.

MAGGIE. Not at all.

MAN IN PAJAMAS. It was your hair. It's very lovely.

MAGGIE. Uh, thank you.

MAN IN PAJAMAS. Yes ... *(To himself as he moves away.)* I've always thought it was so very lovely. *(Maggie watches him walk away.)*

NURSE. You were saying?

MAGGIE. Uh, yes. Maggy Burroughs. I wonder if you could give her this. *(She hands the Nurse a wrapped box.)*

NURSE. Sure. Don't you want to see her?

MAGGIE. Oh, I'm sure she can't have visitors.

NURSE. Yes, she can. She's down in X-ray, but she'll be back soon. Why don't you wait?

MAGGIE. Oh, I really don't want to bother her.

NURSE. You won't be bothering her. I'm sure she'd love to see you.

MAGGIE. Gosh, I'd love to, I really would. But I'm on such a tight schedule.

NURSE. Why don't I just call down there and see when she —

MAGGIE. No! *(Attempting calmness.)* No, thanks a lot but I really just wanted to drop this off. I'll be calling her from New York, though. Maybe you can tell her that. I'll call.

NURSE. *(She's seen this before.)* Right. You'll call.

MAGGIE. *(To audience.)* Don't look at me like that. *(She walks to an area with a table upon which are piled a number of books. To audience.)* I went to my book signing that afternoon. *(Three Women and a Man line up to get their books signed.)* Cathy with a C?

FIRST WOMAN. No, a K.

MAGGIE. There you go.

FIRST WOMAN. Thanks, Miss Mulroney. I just want you to know, I've read all of your books, and I think you're terrific.

MAGGIE. Thank you.

FIRST WOMAN. I love your characters. They're so lonely and sad, but they're all trying real hard to understand their lives. I love that.

MAGGIE.   Thank you.

FIRST WOMAN.   Plus they're funny, of course.

MAGGIE.   Of course. *(The Second Woman approaches.)* Hi. How shall I make this out?

SECOND WOMAN.   Just say, "To my best friend Christine."

MAGGIE.   *(Speaks to audience as she signs the next book.)* I started to wonder, as I often do, why women seem to respond so directly to my stuff. Is there something about sad people you can laugh at that appeals more directly to the female psyche? Not that men don't respond, they do.

YOUNG MAN.   I like the way you interweave the development of the theme with the exterior schematic.

MAGGIE.   Thank you. *(To audience.)* But not in such a personal way. Still, it's nice to have an audience. I'm probably one of the few people who enjoys book signings. All these people who think they know you, and like what they think they know. *(She stands, moves away from the table.)* The whole time I kept coming back to thoughts of Maggy. What were they doing to her? Was chemo painful? What was she feeling right now? *(The phone rings. Maggie walks over to an area with a bed, and picks up the phone on the bedside table.)* Hello?

JIM.   *(On phone.)* How did you know?

MAGGIE.   How did I know what?

JIM.   How did you know to buy her a Sugilite? I gave her one a long time ago, and she lost it. I kept wanting to buy her a new one, but she said there was a reason crystals went away from you, and a reason they came back.

MAGGIE.   You mean she believes in that stuff?

JIM.   Yeah, she does. You must, too, huh? Or you wouldn't have bought her one.

MAGGIE.   … Yeah, yeah, well, you know they have great healing powers.

JIM.   She's sorry she missed you. Evidently you had just left when she came back from X-ray.

MAGGIE.   Oh, what a shame. *(Guilty look at audience.)* How is she?

JIM.   She's doing okay. They were giving her something for the nausea, but she hated it so much she finally told them to stop giving it to her. So now she's doing the whole thing cold turkey. Everyone's amazed.

MAGGIE.   Wow. Are you at the hospital?

JIM.   Yeah. But I'm going home in awhile. It's been a long day.

MAGGIE.   Is there anything I can do? Make you dinner, maybe? I make a mean chicken cacciatore.

JIM.   Thanks, but what I really need is a good night's sleep.

MAGGIE.   Oh. Okay.

JIM.   Take a raincheck? How much longer are you staying in town?

MAGGIE.   Well, I'm not sure. I was going to leave tomorrow.

JIM.   Oh. Too bad.

MAGGIE.   But it's possible I might have to stay in town awhile and do some research.

JIM.   Something new? A new book or something?

MAGGIE.   Maybe, yeah.

JIM.   Oh. Well, good luck.

MAGGIE.   Thanks. *(She hangs up.)* Why did I say that? Research on a new book, that was something that just popped out of my mouth. I really was due to go home tomorrow. I looked around the room of my hotel, with its generic attempt at cheerful decor and realized I needed some air. *(A few people start walking along the street. Maggie joins them. A Daddy and Mommy are pushing a baby carriage.)*

DADDY.   You're going to suffocate her.

MOMMY.   What, you want her to freeze to death?

DADDY.   I want her to be able to breathe.

MOMMY.   She's breathing. Look at her, she's breathing.

DADDY.   How can you tell? I can't even see her in there. *(Maggie peels off, stops. A doorbell sounds and an Older Woman approaches.)*

NORA.   *(Slight Irish accent.)* Yes, may I help you?

MAGGIE.   I saw your Bed and Breakfast sign and was wondering if you had a room available.

NORA.   For how long?

MAGGIE.   I don't know exactly.

NORA.   I see. Well, why don't you come on in? *(Maggie does.)* No bags?

MAGGIE.   They're still at the hotel.

NORA.   Ah. Moving out, are you?

MAGGIE.   Yes. I'm looking for something a little homier.

NORA.   Well, you've come to the right place. This is an old building, some might even call it a shade run down, but I prefer to think of it as homey, just as you say. We serve a continental breakfast from seven to nine, free of charge. And there's a TV room on the first floor. I'm afraid there's no TV in it at the moment.

MAGGIE.   That's fine. I'll take a room.

NORA.   *(Entering her name in the register.)* Your name?

MAGGIE.   Maggie Mulroney.

NORA.   Mulroney, is it? Your family wouldn't hail from County Kerry, would they?

MAGGIE.   I don't really know. My father told me, but I forgot, and now I can't ask.

NORA.   Ah. Passed away, is he, your father?

MAGGIE.   Uh, yes. When I was eighteen.

NORA.   Pity. My dear father died last year, and I'm still half destroyed. And you only a teenager, you poor thing. And your mother, is she still living?

MAGGIE.   Yes. She lives in Seattle. We don't see each other very often.

NORA.   Why not?

MAGGIE.   Um, I'm not sure. It's just the way things worked out.

NORA.   Oh, Maggie, what a shame. Isn't life the saddest thing?

MAGGIE.   *(To audience.)* For a brief moment, I had the overwhelming urge to climb onto her lap and sob until I got uncontrollable hiccups. Fortunately, I suppressed it.

NORA.   Well, Maggie, I'm giving you my daughter's old room, with the view of the park. The nicest room I have available. Anything you need, you just ask. Nora Delaney's my name. And you'll meet my husband, Howard, at breakfast.

MAGGIE.   Thank you, Nora.

NORA.   You know, I've a feeling, were you to be able to ask, that you hail from County Kerry. I knew some Mulroneys from there, and you definitely favor them. *(Nora exits.)*

MAGGIE.   *(To audience.)* Paying someone to be your family, this could be a whole new untapped market. Instead of hiring a prostitute, businessmen could hire some motherly type to come in and tut-tut over how hard it was at the office. Or to yell, "Get those dirty socks off the floor, ya louse!" depending on your inclination. *(She picks up a suitcase, carries it to her new room. It is a teenaged girl's old bedroom, with flowery wallpaper and one of those white bumpy bedspreads on the bed. Maybe a stuffed animal. Maybe a poster. Kind of sweet.)*

Hmm. Nice. Makes me want to throw a slumber party. *(Sitting on the bed.)* County Kerry. Well, who knows? There was something kind of comforting about this woman suggesting that I might actually belong to a tribe somewhere. *(She bounces on the bed a minute testing the mattress.)*

I considered for a moment calling someone to let them know I was staying. Then I realized there was no one I needed to call, except maybe my publicist. I have to admit, I got a little depressed there for a minute. *(Thinking of Maggy's "no friends" comment.)* Not that I don't have any friends, don't get me wrong. I just couldn't think of who they were at the moment. *(She stretches out on the bed.)*

So. Here I was in a Bed and Breakfast, for no apparent reason. And there was Maggy, Jim's Maggy, lying in a bed across town, with poison dripping into her veins. I lay on the bed for a very long time, trying to figure out the correlation. *(Blackout.)*

**END OF ACT ONE**

# ACT TWO

*In the dark, a phone rings. On the third ring it is answered by a machine.*

JIM'S VOICE.   You've reached the Burroughs residence. Here is the Maggy update as of Thursday: She is responding well to chemo, her condition is stable and we hope to have her back in a few days. Leave your message after the beep, and someone will get back to you. *(There is a beep. The lights come up. Maggie is lying on the bed with her head at the foot of it. On the nightstand beside her is a glass of wine and an empty wine bottle. She is on the phone.)*
MAGGIE.   Hi, Jim. It's Maggie. Maggie Mulroney. Guess what? I'm still here. I know you're at the hospital, but I just wanted to say that I'm thinking of you both, and … and I hope you're really kicking some butt with that chemo. *(Cheerleader.)* Let's go, our team, let's go! 'Bye. *(She hangs up the phone. To herself.)* That was really stupid. *(Blackout. The phone rings again. It is again picked up by a machine.)*
JIM'S VOICE.   Hi, this is the Maggy Burroughs hotline. Maggy went through kind of a slump yesterday, but she's feeling much better today and can actually have visitors. I'm boring her to tears, so feel free to drop in and provide a change of pace. Mass General Health and Racquet Club, Cambridge Street entrance. 'Bye. *(Lights up. Maggie is lolling around on an unmade bed. She holds a young girl's doll in one hand and the phone in the other. During the call she plays casually with the doll's clothing.)*
MAGGIE.   Hi, Jim, it's Maggie again. I've been meaning to drop in on Maggy, but I'm so darn busy. I've got an interview today and things are just crazy around here, so please give her my best and tell her I'm thinking of her. Um, okay, that's about it. 'Bye. *(She hangs up. To audience.)* I know, I know. But everybody tells little white lies on the telephone, don't they? The truth is, I kind of needed some time alone. My first night at the B & B, I bought a bottle of wine, drank it in my room and cried

40

for about three hours. The next day I woke up with a monstrous hangover, walked over to the Charles River and threw things into it to watch them sink. I guess you might say I was going through a melancholy phase. I was on my way to a Bergman film retrospective when suddenly, I remembered I had an interview that afternoon. *(Blackout. Pretentious PBS type music, and lights up. Maggie is in a TV studio. A lugubrious looking man with shadows under his eyes, Raymond Terwilliger, sits opposite her. He speaks to the audience.)*

RAYMOND.   Hello, I'm Raymond Terwilliger, and our guest tonight is Margaret Mulroney, whose book *Joined at the Head* is currently topping the New York *Times* Best Seller list. Miss Mulroney is in town at the moment, and we were lucky enough to get her to drop in to chat with us on *The Best of Boston*. Welcome to the show, Margaret.

MAGGIE.   Thank you, Raymond. A pleasure to be here.

RAYMOND.   You're actually a Boston native, aren't you?

MAGGIE.   Well, not really. I spent my adolescence here, however, which were rather important years for me. The Wonder Years.

RAYMOND.   The Wonder Years?

MAGGIE.   Didn't you eat that bread? Soft, white, easy to roll up into balls and throw in the cafeteria? That's where the TV show gets its name.

RAYMOND.   I'm afraid I don't watch commercial television.

MAGGIE.   Oh. Sorry.

RAYMOND.   *Joined at the Head* has been doing so well in terms of sales, you might say there's something of a Margaret Mulroney ground swell going on these days. To what do you attribute this?

MAGGIE.   I'm not sure. I've seen so many of my contemporaries fall in and out of favor, I would hesitate to attribute a rational explanation to anybody's popularity, least of all my own.

RAYMOND.   Do you think the country has gone into a period of self-examination, and that perhaps you exemplify the recent mood of the country?

MAGGIE.   Okay. That sounds good. Honestly, I don't know. I really liked my last book, and I could have offered you a very convincing explanation for its being a hit. But it wasn't, and this is. Go figure.

RAYMOND. *Joined at the Head* is a searing indictment of the father/daughter relationship. Is your —

MAGGIE. Oh, no.

RAYMOND. I beg your pardon?

MAGGIE. It's not a searing indictment of anything. It's funny.

RAYMOND. Be that as it may. Is your relationship with your father as cancerous as the one between Aggie, the protagonist in your book, and her father?

MAGGIE. Cancerous?

RAYMOND. By that I mean destructive. Noxious. Deadly.

MAGGIE. Are you sure we're talking about the same book?

RAYMOND. Yes, I know, I've read all the kudos — "Hilariously funny," "Delightfully witty," etcetera. But I'm sorry, this reviewer found himself quite literally gasping for air while reading your book, the mood you created was so claustrophobic.

MAGGIE. Oh, dear. I'm very sorry.

RAYMOND. You're sorry your book is so powerful?

MAGGIE. Well, it wasn't my intention to hamper your breathing process. I was only trying to poke fun at some of the foibles of the father/daughter thing.

RAYMOND. And most would say you did exactly that. I'm merely trying to get deeper here, Margaret. To discover the real Margaret Mulroney.

MAGGIE. Is that absolutely necessary?

RAYMOND. What is your relationship with your father?

MAGGIE. Fine. Quite normal. He's deceased, unfortunately, but we were very close when he was alive. I think he would approve of this particular book.

RAYMOND. Is that necessary? That he approve.

MAGGIE. *(Flustered.)* Well, no, of course not. *(Nervous laugh.)* I'm starting to feel like I'm in therapy here. I hope your rates are reasonable.

RAYMOND. It has been said that while your women are fully fleshed out characters, the men in your books tend to be caddish, shallow, selfish, even perverted individuals. Why do you think this is?

MAGGIE.  I wasn't aware that such a thing had been said.

RAYMOND.  Well, surely Maxwell Roundtree couldn't be called a sympathetic character.

MAGGIE.  On the contrary. I'd go out with him.

RAYMOND.  You'd go out with him? An egomaniacal skirt-chaser without a moral bone in his body?

MAGGIE.  He's smart, funny, and successful. What more do you need in a man?

RAYMOND.  *(Pause.)* You're not married, are you?

MAGGIE.  *(Slow burn.)* No, as a matter of fact I'm not.

RAYMOND.  Anyone special in your life?

MAGGIE.  I find it interesting that this question is asked of me so frequently. Tell me, if Saul Bellow were on the show tonight, would you ask him about that "special someone" in his life? I'm just curious.

RAYMOND.  Touché. *(To audience.)* We've been talking to Margaret Mulroney, feminist author of *Joined at the Head.* Tomorrow we'll be talking to Jean Kirkpatrick.

MAGGIE.  I hear she's dating someone really cute these days. Ask her to tell you about him.

RAYMOND.  *(Dourly.)* Ha-ha-ha *(To audience.)* This has been *The Best of Boston. (Blackout. A phone rings in the dark. Lights up on Maggie in her room asleep. She turns on the light and picks up the phone.)*

MAGGIE.  Hello?

MRS. MULRONEY.  Maggie?

MAGGIE.  Who's this?

MRS. MULRONEY.  Who do you think?

MAGGIE.  Mother?

MRS. MULRONEY.  Of course. How are you, darling?

MAGGIE.  How am I? Oh, I'm … fine, I guess.

MRS. MULRONEY.  I saw you on that TV show. That man really raked you over the coals, didn't he?

MAGGIE.  He sure did.

MRS. MULRONEY.  What a terrible person. Why did they let him talk to you like that?

MAGGIE.  It's his job, Mom. I guess he didn't like me.

MRS. MULRONEY.  Well, I wanted to scratch his eyes out. You, however, were adorable.

MAGGIE. Adorable?

MRS. MULRONEY. Absolutely. I love your new haircut. It creates a youthful illusion.

MAGGIE. Mom, what time is it?

MRS. MULRONEY. Oh, who looks at the time when your daughter is — are you ready?

MAGGIE. Ready for what? *(Mrs. Mulroney sings a birthday song culminating in "Happy Birthday, Famous Writer Daughter of Mine," etc. Copyrights being what they are, I leave it to her how the tune of the song should go. During it, Maggie says, "Mom," but not to be deterred, Mrs. Mulroney completes the entire song.)* Thank you.

MRS. MULRONEY. I remember that day vividly. It was the most incredible pain of my entire life.

MAGGIE. Sorry.

MRS. MULRONEY. Wait 'til you have one. You'll see.

MAGGIE. In case you haven't noticed, Mom, it doesn't look like I'll be giving birth any time soon.

MRS. MULRONEY. Never say never. There was an article about you in the Seattle *Times*. Somebody read your book and didn't like it.

MAGGIE. Uh-huh. Well, thanks for sharing.

MRS. MULRONEY. No, listen, I bring it up because the guy was a jackass. Wait 'til you see the article, I'm going to mail it to you, you'll see what I mean. A total jackass. What's your address?

MAGGIE. *(Pause.)* I'm staying at the Copley Plaza. Send it there.

MRS. MULRONEY. What?

MAGGIE. I said, "I'm staying —"

MRS. MULRONEY. No, not you. Your father's talking to me.... What?... Oh, your father wants to wish you a happy birthday.

MAGGIE. *(Pause.)* What?

MRS. MULRONEY. Hold on a second. Here, Bud. *(A slight pause. Then a Man's voice.)*

MR. MULRONEY. Hey, baby, that you?

MAGGIE. ... Dad?

MR. MULRONEY. How's the birthday girl?

MAGGIE.   How did you —?

MR. MULRONEY.   Look, I heard about this lousy review, and I hope you're not going to let some joker from Seattle ruin your birthday. In fact, I tell you what I did for you. I rented out a hall, and you're gonna come out here and read your book *page by page* to all these clowns. We'll make them pay to hear it, and they're gonna love it.

MAGGIE.   Daddy?

MR. MULRONEY.   Because that's the only way to deal with these schmoes. Let them know who's boss. You're a comer, kid. And a comer doesn't let anybody stand in her way.

MAGGIE.   Daddy, you can't....

MR. MULRONEY.   Don't whine, Magpie. You know how I hate it when you whine.

MAGGIE.   I'm not. I just —

MR. MULRONEY.   You wanna make your old man proud of you?

MAGGIE.   Well yeah. But —

MR. MULRONEY.   You're not gonna let them treat you like a loser, are you?

MAGGIE.   Dad —

MR. MULRONEY.   Are you?

MAGGIE.   No, Dad.

MR. MULRONEY.   That's my girl. You're a good one, Magpie. Your mother and I love you very much.

MAGGIE.   I love you, too.

MR. MULRONEY.   Now, I've rented this hall, and we're going to force this stuff down all the nay-sayers throats, and before you know it, they'll be begging for more. My daughter is not a loser!

MAGGIE.   Dad, you can't be doing this.

MR. MULRONEY.   What do you mean? I've already sold the tickets, called the newspapers —

MAGGIE.   I mean, you can't be talking to me on the phone right now.

MR. MULRONEY.   Why not?

MAGGIE.   Well, I mean ... you're dead, Dad. *(Long pause.)* Dad? Daddy? *(There is a click.)* Daddy! Daddy, wait! I'm sorry, I didn't mean it! Come back! Daddy, please, talk to me! *(There's a knock at the door. Nora enters.)*

NORA.  Maggie? Are you all right?

MAGGIE.  Uh, yes.

NORA.  I hope you don't mind my barging in on you, but I couldn't help hearing —

MAGGIE.  No, No. Sorry. I ... I embarrassed my father.

NORA.  How's that?

MAGGIE.  In my dream. I think I really embarrassed him. By pointing out that he was dead.

NORA.  Oh. Yes. He probably considered it bad form. Mine does, too. Would you like me to fix you a cup of tea? It might calm your nerves a bit.

MAGGIE.  No, thank you, Nora. I'm sorry to have woken you.

NORA.  Oh, you didn't wake me, it's still early yet. Howard and I were playing Scrabble. Terrible cheater, Howard. He's probably trading in his tiles as we speak.

MAGGIE.  Oh, dear.

NORA.  You know, this may not be the best time to mention it, but there certainly are a lot of phone messages piling up for you downstairs.

MAGGIE.  I know.

NORA.  Your publicist, your editor, a man from the Boston *Globe*. Sounds like a fascinating existence, being a writer.

MAGGIE.  Did anyone call who said they were a friend?

NORA.  Well, not specifically, dear, but I'm sure many of them were. *(Pause.)* I should be getting back to Howard. Will you be all right?

MAGGIE.  Yes, I'm fine. Thanks for looking in.

NORA.  Of course. Tell your father not to take things so seriously.

MAGGIE.  I will. Goodnight. *(Nora exits. Maggie looks at the audience.)* This is getting kind of confusing. I didn't mean to get into all this stuff about my family, it just kind of slipped out. I hope you'll bear with me, sometimes you just veer off track a little, you know? So let's get back to the important stuff. I called Maggy and Jim's house frequently. *(She dials.)*

JIM'S VOICE.  This is the Maggy Burroughs hotline. If all goes well —(*Maggie hangs up.*)

MAGGIE.   But all I got was the machine. It was frustrating. I was feeling kind of nervous and edgy and didn't know what to do about it. I asked myself — What could I do to calm myself down? (*Lights up on Maggie in a Doctor's office. She is buttoning up her blouse. The Doctor is looking at a chart.*)

DOCTOR.   Well, you seem to check out okay. Blood levels normal, heart good, mammography negative. You're in good health.

MAGGIE.   I don't know. I'm not sleeping very well lately.

DOCTOR.   You have a slight tendency towards anemia, but nothing to worry about. Pop a few folic acid tabs now and then.

MAGGIE.   "Pop a few folic acid tabs?"

DOCTOR.   Yeah, sure, what the hell.

MAGGIE.   And what about the headaches?

DOCTOR.   Ever heard of aspirin?

MAGGIE.   Yes, I've heard of aspirin, but what if it's more than a headache? What if it's something serious?

DOCTOR.   You want me to run a CAT scan? I'll be happy to run a CAT scan.

MAGGIE.   Why? You think I need one?

DOCTOR.   I just told you. I think you're perfectly normal. Physically.

MAGGIE.   Then why do you want to run a CAT scan?

DOCTOR.   I don't. I'm humoring you.

MAGGIE.   Look, I'm a little nervous, okay? I just don't feel up to par. Isn't it possible that you missed something?

DOCTOR.   Well, of course, that's always possible. I gave someone a clean bill of health once and he dropped dead the next day.

MAGGIE.   What?

DOCTOR.   But it's very unusual. We can't know everything.

MAGGIE.   This isn't comforting. Somehow I'm not feeling better for this experience.

DOCTOR.   Have you thought about maybe taking a vacation?

MAGGIE.   I'm *on* vacation. Sort of.

DOCTOR.   I see. Well then, perhaps you should go back to work.

MAGGIE.   Have I told you how helpful you've been? You've really been wonderfully helpful.

DOCTOR.   My pleasure. Drop in any time.

MAGGIE.   *(A long, confused pause. Then, to audience.)* You know what? I'm lost. I'm sorry, I thought I knew what I was doing here, but I don't. I'm very embarrassed, I shouldn't have gotten you all out here on false pretenses. So I tell you what — let's just stop here. Maybe a little time away from this will clear my head. *(Maggy enters.)*

MAGGY.   WHAT are you doing?

MAGGIE.   I'm sending everybody home.

MAGGY.   Why?

MAGGIE.   Because I'm lost. I don't know where I'm going. I thought I did, I thought this was going to be a moving tribute to you, and now all this other stuff is coming out.

MAGGY.   What other stuff?

MAGGIE.   About me. Who needs it?

MAGGY.   Evidently you do.

MAGGIE.   No. I don't. It's immaterial. It's off the point. *(To audience.)* 'Bye, everybody. Thanks for your patience and your —

MAGGY.   Don't anybody move! *(To Maggie.)* This is ridiculous. Tell your story.

MAGGIE.   I can't. What are you doing here, anyway? You said you'd never interrupt again.

MAGGY.   Well, obviously I spoke prematurely. I had no idea you'd try to pull a stunt like this. This is highly irresponsible. You owe it to these people to continue. Now talk.

MAGGIE.   No.

MAGGY.   Okay then, I will.

MAGGIE.   *You* will?

MAGGY.   Somebody's got to.

MAGGIE.   But not you. It's my story.

MAGGY.   But you're not telling it. And you can't just leave a story dangling like this. It's extremely bad manners. *(To audience.)* Okay, when last we left our heroine —

MAGGIE.   I'm not the heroine. You are the heroine.

MAGGY.   Oh. What are you?

MAGGIE.   I'm the narrator. My life serves as the backdrop for

48

your story.

MAGGY. Oh. Okay. When we last left our backdrop, she had just come back from a trip to the doctor, which is something about 99% of all people do when they find out someone they know has cancer. She had decided to stay on in Boston in order to be near Jim and me. She then proceeded to avoid us for the next three days.

MAGGIE. What do you mean? I didn't avoid you. I called constantly.

MAGGY. But you never came to the hospital once.

MAGGIE. I was busy!

MAGGY. I see.

MAGGIE. I was! I had an interview, and meetings with —

MAGGY. Excuse me. I'm trying to tell a story here. Do you mind? Thank you. You also saw a dream about a rather strange phone call from her parents.

MAGGIE. Which I ask you to disregard.

MAGGY. Although I myself found it rather interesting. Then, let's see, right after that I came home. It was nice to be back home after five days of staring at the same walls at Mass General, but I felt like total shit. I had mucositis, which is like fifty zillion canker sores all along the lining of your mouth and down your throat. It was the worst. *(She lies on a sofa. Jim enters carrying a milk shake with a straw in it.)*

JIM. Here you go. *(He kneels down, hands her the drink.)* Do you think you can have a little of this? Try to take a sip. *(Painfully, Maggy takes a small sip. Just the act of swallowing is excruciating. She pushes it away and reaches for a pillow.)* Let me get that for you. *(He puts it behind her back.)* How're you feeling?

MAGGY. A little achy.

JIM. You could be run over by a steamroller, and as they peeled you off the pavement and asked you how you felt, you'd say, "Oh, a little achy." C'mon, drink this.

MAGGY. Jim, please, go away.

JIM. Sorry, I'm here for good. Get used to it. Now drink. *(She takes a sip.)* Thank you. It's good to have you home, sweetie.

MAGGY. It's good to be home.

JIM. You look wonderful.

MAGGY.  Oh, please.

JIM.  What?

MAGGY.  I look like shit, let's face it.

JIM.  You look alive. That's wonderful enough for me.

MAGGY.  Did you think I was going to die?

JIM.  Of course not.

MAGGY.  It could happen, you know. You should be prepared for that.

JIM.  Why are you getting so morbid? You're home, we won this round. Things are looking up.

MAGGY.  You're a hopeless optimist, you know that?

JIM.  You're still here. You're control group's not. You think that's not cause for optimism?

MAGGY.  Oh, yeah. I think about all my dead friends, and it just cheers me right up. Thank you for reminding me. *(The phone rings. Jim picks it up.)*

JIM.  Speak.

MAGGIE.  Oh, Jim! I thought I'd get your machine.

JIM.  We just got home.

MAGGIE.  How's Maggy feeling?

JIM.  Pretty well under the circumstances.

MAGGIE.  I'm so glad. Can I talk to her?

JIM.  Not at the moment. She's kind of lying low.

MAGGIE.  Sure, yeah, of course. Well, I just wanted to check in on you and see how things were. Let you know I'm thinking of you.

JIM.  That's nice of you, Mag. Thanks.

MAGGIE.  And, you know, if there's anything I can do....

JIM.  Thanks. When she's feeling better, we'd like to have you out to dinner.

MAGGIE.  That would be great. Well, love to Maggy. *(She hangs up. Lights up on her.)*

JIM.  Maggie sends her love. She left about twenty-five messages on the machine while you were in the hospital.

MAGGY.  You didn't call her back?

JIM.  No. Too busy.

MAGGY.  Jim, call her back. Go out with her. Have some fun.

JIM.  I don't want to. I want to be with you.

MAGGY.   You are with me, almost every minute you're not at school. You deserve a break.

JIM.   Why should I get a break? You don't get one.

MAGGY.   Well, maybe I need one, too.

JIM.   What, from me?

MAGGY.   All this cheerfulness is really depressing me. Why don't you go out with her and be yourself for a while?

JIM.   I don't know what you're talking about. I am being myself.

MAGGY.   *(Sighs.)* Okay.

JIM.   You don't think I'm being myself?

MAGGY.   Sure. I'm just a little cranky. Forget about it.

JIM.   *(Pause.)* Are you going to drink this?

MAGGY.   No. I can't.

JIM.   Sure, you can. Look, one more sip, then I promise I'll leave you alone for twenty minutes.

MAGGY.   You just don't give up, do you?

JIM.   Nope. I'm relentless. I was a Yorkshire terrier in another life. *(Maggy smiles.)* Ah, I've got her smiling. Let me take advantage of this rare moment of mirth. Drink, madam, or you'll get dehydrated.

MAGGY.   *(Standing and approaching audience.)* And that's exactly what did happen. I got dehydrated, and it was back to the hospital for me. Interestingly, Maggie still did not visit, although she sent many strange and exotic gifts. Jim did, however, finally return her calls, and the next night they had dinner at our house.

MAGGIE.   We don't need to do that.

MAGGY.   What?

MAGGIE.   The dinner. It was just one of those old time's sake kind of dinners, and it had nothing to do with you.

MAGGY.   Hey, who's telling this story?

MAGGIE.   I don't see how you could possibly tell a story about a dinner you weren't at.

MAGGY.   Maybe I'll surprise you.

MAGGIE.   I'd rather you didn't.

MAGGY.   Come on. You're stuck, I might as well take a stab at this, don't you think? *(Silence.)* Okay. *(To audience.)* Maggie went over to dinner at our house the night I went back to the hospital. Here's what I think probably happened. *(Lights up on Jim and Maggie. Jim is playing a tune on the piano, a beautiful lyrical song with no words. \*)*

MAGGIE.   Jim, that's beautiful.

JIM.   You really like it?

MAGGIE.   Oh God, yes.

JIM.   I wrote it for Maggy.

MAGGIE.   Really? She must have been so touched.

JIM.   Yeah. She likes it. Do you remember this? *(He plays a song from an earlier time. A less mature attempt at a love song.)*

MAGGIE.   I thought you might have forgotten that one.

JIM.   How could I forget the first love song I ever wrote? You were such a lovely girl. You still are.

MAGGIE.   Oh, no.

JIM.   Yes, you are. You know, I feel I could only say this to you, and please try not to judge me — it's such a relief to be with someone who's healthy. God, I hate myself for saying that. But poor Maggy, I feel like I have to be so careful with her all the time. She's so fragile, it's like being with a wounded bird. I broke one of her ribs once making love, just snapped it in two. And we were both trying to be so careful, it was like making love to a teacup. But I broke her rib anyway. I heard it break.

MAGGIE.   Oh Jim, how horrible.

JIM.   Maggie, sometimes I wonder how much more of this I can take. And then I hate myself, because she's the one who's going through the pain. What the fuck right do I have to cave in?

MAGGIE.   *(Taking his hand.)* You're not caving in, Jim. It's hard. No one comes out a hero at a time like this. It's hard.

JIM.   Come here. *(She moves toward him. He kisses her. She responds.)* Please forgive me. *(He kisses her again.)* Please, please forgive me. *(They are in each other's arms, obviously on their way to other things.)*

MAGGIE.   *(Murmuring, to Jim.)* No ... no ... no.... *(Breaking away; to Maggy.)* No, no, NO! You've got it all wrong. God! How

* See Special Note on Original Music on copyright page.

52

could you even think such a thing?

MAGGY.   How could I think such a thing? Isn't that where all this has been leading?

MAGGIE.   No! Jesus, Maggy, give me a little credit. Or forget me, give Jim a little credit. He would no sooner have made a pass at me than he would have cut off his arm.

MAGGY.   Really?

MAGGIE.   Of course, really. Honestly! You really shock me sometimes.

MAGGY.   Well then, what happened? If he didn't make a pass at you, what happened?

MAGGIE.   I really don't want to get into it.

MAGGY.   I think you'd better, don't you? To clear up this misconception.

MAGGIE.   It has nothing to do with this story, Maggy, it's extraneous and completely off the track.

MAGGY.   What track? I thought you were stuck.

MAGGIE.   *(Pause.)* All right, all right, I'll try to encapsulate it.

MAGGY.   Good. *(She exits.)*

MAGGIE.   *(To audience.)* I went to dinner at Jim's that night. I'll make this quick, then we'll move on to other things. *(Maggie moves into position next to Jim, who is again playing the love song to Maggy.*)* Maybe the problem was that I'd had too much wine with dinner. I always tend to take life too seriously when I have wine in my system. Everything seems so goddamn meaningful. *(Jim's song comes to a close.)* Jim, that's beautiful.

JIM.   You like it?

MAGGIE.   Oh God, yes.

JIM.   I wrote it for Maggy.

MAGGIE.   I had a feeling. You're so talented. I always thought you were going to end up being a famous musician.

JIM.   Instead of a loser high school teacher?

MAGGIE.   Jim, that's not what I —

JIM.   Hey, I'm kidding. Look, there was a time when I thought so, too. You and I always vowed we'd get out of this place and make good. You're the one who did it.

MAGGIE.   Are you sorry you didn't?

* See Special Note on Original Music on copyright page.

JIM. I was at first. Then I met Maggy. I wouldn't change a thing now — except for this little cancer thing, which is kind of cramping our style.

MAGGIE. *(Pause.)* Would you like to talk about that? I mean, I just want you to know that I'm here for you if you want to —

JIM. Thanks. No. I'm fine.

MAGGIE. The other night in the car —

JIM. Little moment of insanity, Mag.

MAGGIE. That wasn't insanity, that was a perfectly natural response to a terrible situation.

JIM. It's nothing to worry about. Hope you'll forget it happened.

MAGGIE. It was good it happened. I'm just glad I was the one you chose to —

JIM. Maggie, I didn't choose anything. You just happened to be there, okay? No big deal. *(Pause.)* Hey, remember this one? *(Jim plays the second song.\*)*

MAGGIE. *(To audience.)* I couldn't believe it. First he pulls the rug out from under me, then he tries to make up for it by playing me a love song. *(An edge in her voice. To Jim.)* Yeah, that's pretty. Play that Van Morrison tune I used to like.

JIM. *(Stopping.)* What?

MAGGIE. What was it called? "Blue Money" or something?

JIM. You're kidding me, right?

MAGGIE. Why would I be kidding?

JIM. I'm playing a love song I wrote you almost twenty years ago and you tell me to play Van Morrison?

MAGGIE. I like that song, I really do. But you just said it, times change. I mean, look at us. We're hardly teenagers anymore. It's kind of embarrassing.

JIM. This is vintage you, you know that? Christ! You haven't changed a bit.

MAGGIE. Why is it vintage me? What do you mean?

JIM. Oh, forget it.

MAGGIE. No, I want to know. Why is it vintage me?

JIM. You always used to do this, Maggie, always. How many

\* See Special Note on Original Music on copyright page.

54

times did I have to tell you, you do not stop someone in the middle of a song?

MAGGIE. Well I'm sorry, but I was just —

JIM. I don't care! It is so fucking rude. Not to mention controlling.

MAGGIE. Oh, *I'm* controlling? That's very funny from someone who always had to call the shots.

JIM. Oh, yeah. Turn it around. Now it's my fault.

MAGGIE. It is! It's been the pattern from the beginning. Who dumped who at the senior prom?

JIM. The senior prom again. Maggie, I wasn't going to mention this, but since you keep on bringing it up — I didn't dump you at the senior prom. You dumped me.

MAGGIE. I did not!

JIM. Yes, you did. You don't remember this? You told me your father had always said I was a loser, and you didn't want to be saddled with a loser for the rest of your life.

MAGGIE. I never said that!

JIM. Yes, you did. Believe me, Mag, it's not the kind of thing a guy forgets.

MAGGIE. *(To audience.)* A loser. Oh, my God, I probably did say that.

JIM. Maybe that's why I ran off that night with Gina Lazlo.

MAGGIE. Jim, I'm so sorry. I don't know how I could have been so cruel.

JIM. Your dad had just died. You were having a hard time. I was a moody musician with pipe dreams of grandeur and very little compassion. Who wouldn't have dumped me?

MAGGIE. You're awfully understanding.

JIM. Only in retrospect. To tell you the truth, I was pretty pissed off there for a couple of years. After Maggy got sick, though, I looked back on that time and realized what was really going on with you. It's a bitch. There's no way around it.

MAGGIE. I know. I wish you'd allow yourself to be comforted a little, Jim. This New England stoicism is so unhealthy.

JIM. Hey, don't talk to me about what's unhealthy, okay? I don't remember you being so warm and wonderful while your dad was wasting away. *(Pause.)* Christ, that was a low blow. I don't know why, but being around you seems to strike a raw nerve in me. That's why I haven't been returning your calls.

MAGGIE. Oh. I hadn't realized you didn't want to talk to me. I thought you were just too busy.

JIM. I was. Oh, God, Mag. Don't take this as rejection.

MAGGIE. I'm trying not to. Give me a minute.

JIM. I just can't talk about this. Cancer, Mag! You must remember what that's like.

MAGGIE. *(Pause.)* Yes, I do. *(Her voice breaking.)* And I'm really sorry.

JIM. Oh, boy. Just like old times, huh? *(He puts his arm around her.)* I'm being an asshole.

MAGGIE. And I'm being hypersensitive. It's a magic combination, isn't it. I feel just like I'm sixteen again. I hated being sixteen.

JIM. *(Raymond Terwilliger.)* Ah, The Wonder Years.

MAGGIE. Oh, no. You didn't see that interview, did you?

JIM. 'Fraid so.

MAGGIE. Oh, *no.* I was desperately hoping no one ever watched that show.

JIM. It's big with hospital waiting rooms. Good soporific. Listen, the guy's a moron. You should have seen him with Larry Bird.

MAGGIE. Do you think he's right about my book?

JIM. Well, I think he's right that your father would approve.

MAGGIE. What's that supposed to mean? *(Jim shrugs.)* You don't like that book, do you?

JIM. Hey, who am I to judge? It's selling like hotcakes, everybody loves it —

MAGGIE. What's wrong with it? Come on, Jim, you're an English teacher. You're one of the most perceptive people I've ever known. Since I've endowed you with the power to make me listen to you, you might as well take advantage of it and tell me what's wrong. *(Pause.)*

JIM. Okay. In my opinion, it's dishonest.

MAGGIE. Dishonest.

JIM. It's not your dad. It's some swell guy that you cooked up in order to make America laugh, but it's not your dad. Now if that was your intention, fine, then you succeeded. But if you were trying to capture your dad and the essence of your relationship with him, well, I didn't buy it.

MAGGIE. I see. Well, what did you want me to write? That I was a delinquent teenager who never lived up to his expectations? That he died before I could ever make him proud of me?

JIM. If that's the truth, yes.

MAGGIE. Oh, yeah, that sounds fascinating. The story of one woman's failure. That'll sell millions for sure.

JIM. Well, you're right. I suppose if selling millions is what you're after, you might have to dress it up a bit.

MAGGIE. It's so easy to be righteous from a distance, isn't it?

JIM. Maggie, I'm not judging you, I'm really not. I'm just surprised to see the old firebrand I knew turning out such innocuous stuff. Sorry. *(Maggie gets up.)* You're mad at me, right?

MAGGIE. This is just a little more honesty than I can take in one evening.

JIM. Mag, I'm your friend. What am I supposed to do, lie to you?

MAGGIE. I'm your friend, too. But once every twenty years seems like just about enough right now.

JIM. Are you going?

MAGGIE. Yeah. It's late, anyway. Thanks for dinner. I'd better get home.

JIM. Maggie. *(She turns.)* I was looking forward to showing you the great guy I've turned into. How happy ten years of marriage has made me, how I finally managed to acquire some compassion along the way. I'm sorry I screwed it up.

MAGGIE. *(Pause.)* You didn't screw it up, Jim. *You* did just fine. *(Maggie gets in the car and starts to drive. Soon she is sobbing. Maggy enters and gets into the seat next to her.)*

MAGGY. How come everybody in this story seems to cry in their cars?

MAGGIE. Leave me alone.

MAGGY. This is very reckless driving, Maggie. You're on Lamarr Street driving like an idiot.

MAGGIE. Who cares? We're all just gonna die anyway.

MAGGY.    Oh, that's a fine attitude, I must say. Come on. I know you're upset, but this is your car and someone's got to drive it. Pull yourself together, Mag. Please. *(Maggie stops crying. She begins to concentrate on driving the car.)* Thanks. You were making me nervous.

MAGGIE.    I told you we didn't need that scene! Your name was barely mentioned!

MAGGY.    I was there, though. I was clearly there.

MAGGIE.    What was I looking for from him? Why didn't I get it?

MAGGY.    Maybe you did get it and just didn't realize it.

MAGGIE.    What do you mean?

MAGGY.    What do you think you were looking for?

MAGGIE.    Approval. As usual. The never ending quest for approval.

MAGGY.    And all you got was friendship. Tough break. *(She stands.)* Well, 'bye.

MAGGIE.    Are you leaving?

MAGGY.    Yeah. I think you're back on track now. Drive carefully, will you? You could kill yourself driving like that. *(She exits.)*

MAGGIE.    *(To audience.)* So anyway, where was I? Oh, yes. Maggy was doing about as well as could be expected, according to the hospital, and ... and I was still scared to visit her. But she was due to come home the next day, so I.... Listen, let's do this another way. Here are all the things that happened from this point on. This story is just going to have to tell itself. *(The phone rings. Maggie picks it up.)* Hello?

JIM.    Maggy's worse. An infection has set in, she's running a high fever. *(Pause.)* Hello?

MAGGIE.    Yes, I'm here. *(Blackout. Lights up on the hospital. Maggie enters carrying a plastic bonsai tree. She walks up to the front desk.)* Excuse me.

NURSE.    Yes?

MAGGIE.    I wanted to check on the condition of one of your patients. Margaret Burroughs.

NURSE.    *(Paging though files.)* Burroughs. I'm sorry, she's passed away.

58

MAGGIE.   What?

NURSE.   *(Pause.)* Oh, no, wait. That's Burris. Margaret Burroughs. Stable. Sorry about that. Haven't had my morning coffee.

MAGGIE.   Please have it now.

JIM.   *(Entering.)* Maggie! *(He takes her by the arm, leads her away from desk.)* It's good to see you.

MAGGIE.   How is she?

JIM.   She's being pumped full of antibiotics. She really gave us a scare, but the doctor says she'll be fine.

MAGGIE.   Oh, what a relief.

JIM.   It's amazing how quickly she bounces back from these things. She's got a lot of fight in her, that girl. But hey, I'm sorry to have dragged you out here in the middle of the night.

MAGGIE.   No. I'm glad you called. I ... I have very strong memories of this place.

JIM.   You do?

MAGGIE.   I used to visit my father here.

JIM.   Oh. Well hey, Mag, you don't need to stick around. I'll tell Maggy you dropped by and —

MAGGIE.   No. I'd like to see her. I mean, if she can handle visitors.

JIM.   Yeah, she can. In fact, she asked for you. She thinks you're a kindred spirit.

MAGGIE.   Are you okay? You look exhausted.

JIM.   I'm fine, I'm fine. Why don't you go on in? It's Room 36. I'll be in in a minute.

MAGGIE.   Okay. Listen, about last night —

JIM.   Magpie, let's do ourselves a favor and forget about last night.

MAGGIE.   *(Smiling.)* Magpie. You call Maggy that, too?

JIM.   No, that one's yours. All yours. Now get on in there.

MAGGIE.   Thanks. *(She exits. Jim's face goes from hopeful and encouraging to a mask of grief. He goes over to a water fountain. Washes his face as he drinks from it. Straightens up and looks at the audience.)*

JIM.   Here's what you won't hear from them about me. You won't hear about the nights I lie awake looking at Maggy, thinking about what a wonderful mother she would have made. Or

59

how beautiful our children would have been. You won't hear about how I lust for her, even now, even with tubes running out of her body. How I fantasize about making her well with my ejaculations, as though it were a life-giving fluid that could wash through her entire body and render her clean again. Or about the other side of that, the self-hatred that goes along with forcing yourself upon a sick person. Even though she pretends it's voluntary, that she wants it, too. You won't hear about the anger, an anger so strong and vicious it feels like it could wipe out cities. Anger at the world, at fate, at this fucking roll of the dice that is your life. And anger at Maggy, for letting herself get so sick. For doing this to me and ruining my life. You particularly won't hear about this last because I don't tell it to anyone, least of all myself. You won't hear about my dreams, dreams of flight, of other women, of another life, the one with her we didn't get to have. You won't know what comfort I take in these dreams, the true happiness I find in them. And the strange sensation of waking up to discover that it's your life that is the nightmare, not the dream. "Don't cry, Jim, it's only your life. You're asleep now, everything's okay." You won't hear about the people I work with, and how they've reacted to all this. How some are compassionate and caring, and others treat me like I'm perhaps a carrier and they're going to get it themselves. Still others act as though nothing has happened, and I'm probably overreacting. And more than one woman is already shooting up flares — "I'm available when all this is over!" Vulture women. If they knew my fantasies regarding them, every sphincter would open in abject fear. You won't hear about the effort it takes to stay positive, to keep hoping, to never let her know I've given up. And you won't know, because she couldn't possibly realize herself, how desperately and deeply I love her. My partner. My life partner. The one I'm joined to forever. My love. My wife. *(He takes another drink from the water fountain, slicks back his hair.)* I just thought you should know. *(He exits. The lights come up on Maggy. She is lying in bed with her eyes closed, listening to music from a tape recorder. Maggie enters.)*

MAGGIE. Maggy?

MAGGY. Hey! Come on in. Don't be shy. You look like you

think I'm going to drop dead before your eyes.

MAGGIE.   Actually, I think you look pretty good. I mean, you don't look ready for the Olympics, but you look better than I imagined.

MAGGY.   Kind of makes me wonder what you imagined.

MAGGIE.   How do you feel?

MAGGY.   Fine. A little achy. *(Looking at the gift.)* What is that?

MAGGIE.   I don't know. I found it in the gift shop.

MAGGY.   I hope you weren't planning on giving it to me.

MAGGIE.   No, no. I've been really needing something like this for my apartment. *(They laugh.)* I keep buying you the most ridiculous things. I don't know why.

MAGGY.   They're not ridiculous! *(She pulls a Walkman from under her pillow.)* I've been listening to these tapes all day. They're great.

MAGGIE.   What do they say?

MAGGY.   Oh, there's nature sounds, and subliminal messages. "You're feeling better every minute," that kind of stuff.

MAGGIE.   I never trusted those things. I'm always afraid they're really saying something like "Kill the landlord."

MAGGY.   But you got it for me anyway.

MAGGIE.   Well, yeah.

MAGGY.   And what about my crystal?

MAGGIE.   Oh, the crystal's different. Those things are potent.

MAGGY.   *(Laughing.)* Oh, no, what have I reduced you to? Buying gifts that go against all your convictions and then pretending you believe in them.

MAGGIE.   Well, you never know.

MAGGY.   No, you never really do. *(Pause.)* Why don't you sit down? You're making me nervous.

MAGGIE.   Oh. Okay. *(She sits.)*

MAGGY.   This is hard for you, isn't it?

MAGGIE.   No, no! *(Pause.)* Well, a little. It's been a long time since I've been in a hospital.

MAGGY.   You didn't have to come, Maggie.

MAGGIE.   *(Seriously.)* Yes, I did. *(Pause.)* I want to hear that story!

MAGGY.   What stor — oh, that story.

61

MAGGIE.    About that big moment in your life. About me being your inspiration.

MAGGY.   Oh, yeah. I probably shouldn't have mentioned that.

MAGGIE.   Why not?

MAGGY.   Well, it makes me feel a little guilty. Sometimes I feel like a big impostor.

MAGGIE.   What do you mean?

MAGGY.   *(Beat.)* Jim and I first met at a Fourth of July parade, did he tell you that?

MAGGIE.   Uh-huh.

MAGGY.   He was standing there watching the floats, and I kind of sidled over and stood next to him. I remembered him from school. In fact, I remembered him as your boyfriend. It was surprising to see him standing there by himself all those years later, looking sort of lost and lonely. I just assumed he'd married you and gone off to become a big shot somewhere — you know, Brown Book Award and all.

MAGGIE.   *(Smiling.)* Yeah.

MAGGY.   Anyway, there I stood next to Jim looking at the parade, feeling kind of stupid, and here's what I thought: "If I were Maggie Mulroney right now, what would I say?"

MAGGIE.   Uh-oh.

MAGGY.   And at that moment a float went by with Gina Lazlo on it. She was looking a little the worse for wear — to tell you the truth she kind of peaked in 12th grade. She was all dolled up as some kind of overweight sex goddess on a float that said Bigelow Pontiac — she married Robbie Bigelow, did you know that?

MAGGIE.   No!

MAGGY.   Yes! So here she is on Robbie's float waving a wand, you really had to be there to appreciate the full impact, and I said, "Living proof. You drive 'em off the lot, and they lose their value instantly." *(Maggie laughs.)* Hey, it was a start.

MAGGIE.   No, I like it.

MAGGY.   Yeah, so did he. He looked at me like I'd just arrived on the planet, one of those "what have we here?" looks, you know?

MAGGIE.   Yeah.

MAGGY. And I felt like a million dollars. Suddenly, I had this new personality, and I felt so free and liberated. So from that moment on, I was a different person. Kind of sassy, and wise-cracking, just like your crowd used to be. It was great, I really started to have fun, and I could tell Jim liked it. But after a while I started to worry. I said to myself, "This isn't really you. This is Maggie Mulroney. How long can you keep up being someone else?"

MAGGIE. But Maggy, that's not me. I'm not free and liberated at all.

MAGGY. Oh yes, you are, Maggie. You don't know it, but you are. And I was always so repressed. See, my mother was a serious alcoholic. I mean really, a hopeless wreck of a person, she led a very sad life. I spent all my time trying to make up for her, by being the most perfect little person on God's green earth. That's why I came off like such a priss — But God! I was so angry underneath. At my mother, for taking away my childhood. But mostly at myself, for being such a "good girl," for letting everybody push me around. You don't know how much I wanted to go to that demonstration in Boston with all of you and scream at the top of my lungs, "This is wrong! This is wrong! This is —" *(Her face contorts.)*

MAGGIE. Are you okay?

MAGGY. Where's that bowl? *(Maggie finds the bowl and hands it to her. Maggy dry heaves into it.)* Sorry. Thought I was going to lose it for a minute.

MAGGIE. Do you want the nurse?

MAGGY. No, no. This happens all the time. Don't worry about it, I'm fine.

MAGGIE. A glass of water, maybe?

MAGGY. Sure. Thanks. *(Pause. Maggie pours water from the pitcher on the table and hands it to Maggy.)* Anyway, where was I? Oh, yeah, pretending to be you. I kept telling myself it wasn't that big a deal. Then last week Jim called and said he was bringing you home to meet me. You know what it felt like? It felt like the real Maggie was coming back to town.

MAGGIE. No.

MAGGY. I just couldn't shake that feeling.

MAGGIE.   But Maggie, that's just not true. There is no "real Maggie." There's just you and me. Listen, I was kind of worried before I met you, too. I was thinking to myself, Here's the woman who lived the life I didn't have. Let's see what it's like." Then I met you, and realized how egotistical that was. You're not living the life I didn't have. You're leading your own life, which is unique and distinct from anybody else's. And as for being anything like me — I should only be so lucky. You just blow me away with your strength, and your courage, and your humor in the face of this thing you're going through. You don't remind me of me at all.

MAGGY.   But Maggie, that's exactly what I see in you. Strength, courage, and humor. How can you say we're nothing alike?

MAGGIE.   I don't know.

MAGGY.   I don't think you see yourself very clearly, Mag. You ought to start taking a closer look.

MAGGIE.   I'm trying, I really am. But it's hard, you know? I think it's a writer thing. You spend all your time looking at other people's lives, you get out of the habit of looking at your own.

MAGGY.   No, that's not it.

MAGGIE.   It's not?

MAGGY.   I don't think so.

MAGGIE.   *(Pause.)* No. I'm afraid if I look, I'll see someone I really don't like at all.

MAGGY.   Yeah, that's it.

MAGGIE.   You know that one?

MAGGY.   Oh, yeah. It's a scary one. It hurts like hell for a while, but after that you feel much better.

MAGGIE.   Funny. Isn't that the way you described chemo?

MAGGY.   Yeah, it is. Surviving the cure is the toughest part.

MAGGIE.   I want you to get better, Maggy. I want you to beat this thing.

MAGGY.   I will. Don't you worry, I will. *(Maggie and Maggy embrace. They hold one another for a long moment. Then they release.)*

MAGGIE.   *(Pause.)* It's my birthday today.

MAGGY.   Really? You didn't tell anyone!

MAGGIE. I don't usually celebrate it.

MAGGY. Well, I think it's high time you started. *(She hands her back the weird looking plant Maggie gave her.)* Happy Birthday, Maggie.

MAGGIE. *(As they laugh.)* Thank you, Maggy. I can't think of anyone I'd rather share it with. *(Pause.)* Jim's out there.

MAGGY. I know.

MAGGIE. He tells me we have a reunion coming up, did you know that?

MAGGY. Yeah. I'll go if you go.

MAGGIE. Deal. *(Suddenly she laughs.)*

MAGGY. What?

MAGGIE. I can't believe that Gina Lazlo actually brought you two together.

MAGGY. Hey, there's one good reason to make that reunion right there.

MAGGIE. Check out how much she's depreciated?

MAGGY. You bet.

MAGGIE. Well…. I'll see you, my friend.

MAGGY. My friend, you absolutely will. 'Bye. *(Maggie exits. Jim approaches.)*

JIM. Everything okay?

MAGGIE. Yeah. Yeah, everything's fine. She looks so pale.

JIM. That's temporary. She'll be back on her feet soon.

MAGGIE. Absolutely. *(Silence.)* Well!

JIM. Listen, I'm going to stay with Maggy for a while, but I thought tomorrow we could maybe take a spin around Newbridge. Check out some of the places you haven't seen yet.

MAGGIE. I'd love to, but you know what, Jim? I think I have to go back to New York.

JIM. Oh, I'm sorry. We'll miss you. Finished all your research, huh?

MAGGIE. Yeah, pretty much. It's time to go home and take stock. But listen, I'm planning on seeing you both at that reunion.

JIM. Oh, we wouldn't miss it.

MAGGIE. *(Pause.)* I can see it, you know.

JIM.   What's that?

MAGGIE.   What you were trying to show me last night. The person you've become. I think you're an amazing man, Jim.

JIM.   I don't feel too amazing. I feel pretty goddamned ordinary, if you want to know the truth.

MAGGIE.   Well, you're wrong. To me, you're a great man.

JIM.   *(Hugging her.)* Best of luck to you, Mag.

MAGGIE.   Thanks, Jim. You, too. *(Jim exits. Maggie stands thinking for a moment. Then she looks up at the audience.)* I was just thinking. We are now coming to a part of the story that I wasn't going to get into when I first began, but I see now that it would be kind of dishonest not to. The only thing is, there are a number of ways to go about this. I'm not sure whether a clinical explanation is in order here, perhaps an itemization of the medical procedures —

MAGGY.   *(Sitting up in bed.)* Oh, please, no. That would be really boring.

MAGGIE.   You think?

MAGGY.   Oh, definitely. So far you've managed to avoid technical jargon, it's probably the only reason people are still here.

MAGGIE.   Oh, thanks a lot. Okay, you're so smart, you tell me. How do I do this?

MAGGY.   I don't know. A couple of jokes first, to loosen everybody up?

MAGGIE.   I think jokes would be in bad taste at the moment.

MAGGY.   Maybe you're right. How about a little music? "Adagio for Strings"?

MAGGIE.   "Adagio for Strings?" Now who's romanticizing? *(To audience.)* What Maggy's trying to help me with can actually be said very simply, so I might as well say it. She died.

MAGGY.   Well, that wasn't very imaginative.

MAGGIE.   Sorry. Sometimes it's better to come right out and say it.

MAGGY.   Yeah, but just bang, she died? That's kind of drab, don't you think?

MAGGIE.   I'm just trying to be honest.

MAGGY.   Okay, honest is good. But there are so many more

colorful ways to say it. "Gave up the ghost." "Passed on to a better world." "Shook hands with Elvis."

MAGGIE.   Maggy, I'd like to end this with a little decorum.

MAGGY.   Sorry. You're absolutely right.

MAGGIE.   *(To audience.)* It was six months later. She had another round of chemo, and I guess this one took her just a little too close to the edge. I went to the funeral. Jim was a mess. It was as though everything just broke loose inside him, now that he didn't have to be strong for someone else. We both went to the reunion, but it wasn't much fun. Even though Maggy was in the class behind us, I felt like she belonged there more than either one of us. She would have gotten such a kick out of Gina Lazlo Bigelow, sexpot turned Born Again Christian.

MAGGY.   No!

MAGGIE.   Yes!

MAGGY.   Oh, I wish I could have been there.

MAGGIE.   You'd have loved it. And me…. I took Maggy's death pretty hard, myself. I went back to New York, took one look at my apartment, and decided to move out of the city. I'd had a long standing offer to teach at this college in Iowa which I'd never really taken seriously, an inner voice had always said to me, "Nah, that's a loser thing to do." But for some reason that inner voice had stopped talking. I picked up the phone and told them I'd be out within the week.

MAGGY.   Did it help?

MAGGIE.   It didn't hurt. I wrote a furious novel about women in the nineties which left everyone bewildered. They kept looking for the jokes. But that's another story.

MAGGY.   Please don't tell it now. *(She exits.)*

MAGGIE.   Don't worry, I won't. *(She looks back. Maggy is gone. A pause.)* It's funny, though. I mean funny in retrospect. I keep thinking about the walk back from the cemetery the day of Maggy's funeral. It was another one of those eerily clear days when sound travels like lightening and the sun is like a klieg-light. And I was wrapped up in my own story, I really didn't want to hear anybody else's. But I just couldn't help it, there they were, all around me. *(The same late-afternoon light appears from the first Act. A number of people start to emerge from the wings.)*

MAN. You've got to look at the whole picture. Your problem is that you fragmentize.

WOMAN. I do not. What does that mean, anyway?

MAN. You look at the fragments.

WOMAN. I most certainly do not, and I resent that. *(They exit. Two Women are talking.)*

YOUNGER WOMAN. Oh, we were deeply in love.

OLDER WOMAN. You were? I didn't even know you knew him that well.

YOUNGER WOMAN. Well, I don't, but we had the most incredible weekend. We fell so in love, it was very intense.

OLDER WOMAN. A weekend? That qualifies as being deeply in love?

YOUNGER WOMAN. We totally grokked each other in a Heinlein kind of way.

OLDER WOMAN. I have absolutely no idea what you're talking about. *(They exit. Two Men walk by.)*

FIRST MAN. Do you know what the chances are of that happening again?

SECOND MAN. Nine hundred and eighty-nine to one.

FIRST MAN. Oh, you are such a wise ass.

SECOND MAN. No, really. Nine hundred and eighty-nine to one.

FIRST MAN. How could you possibly calculate such a thing?

SECOND MAN. Okay, there's nine players on a team; right?

FIRST MAN. Yeah.

SECOND MAN. And nine planets. Also there are seven days in the week, right?

FIRST MAN. Yeah, yeah, yeah. This is bullshit.

SECOND MAN. No, listen. How many cards in a deck? *(They exit. For a moment, Maggie is alone.)*

MAGGIE. *(To audience.)* I couldn't help listening to their conversations. Everyone with his own story. Each person deeply involved in her own activity. And it was the events of the day, I guess. Suddenly it all seemed to be too much. I'm afraid I started to feel very, very sorry for myself. Because I couldn't help noticing that while everyone else seemed to be in the company of another person or persons, I seemed to be the only person on the whole street who was walking entirely alone. *(During the previous, the people have reemerged, walking in couples, threes. As they move offstage, one of them peels away and joins Maggie, who is walking in the opposite direction. She is Maggy, without the scarf, with a full head of shining hair. Maggie sees her. They smile. Together, they walk directly into the light. Blackout.)*

### END OF PLAY

# PROPERTY LIST

Engagement ring (ENGAGED WOMAN)
Bottle of red wine (MAGGY)
Wine glasses (JIM)
Yearbook (JIM)
Bag (MAGGIE)
Notebook (MAGGIE)
Pen/pencil (MAGGIE)
Drinks (WAITER)
3 menus (WAITER)
Coats (COAT CHECK GIRL)
Sugilite crystal (SALESMAN)
Wrapped box (MAGGIE)
IV stand with wheels (MAN IN PAJAMAS)
*Joined at the Head* books (MAGGIE)
Suitcase (MAGGIE)
Empty wine bottle (MAGGIE)
Doll (MAGGIE)
Milkshake with straw (JIM)
Plastic bonsai tree (MAGGIE)
Walkman tape recorder (MAGGY)
Hospital bowl (MAGGIE)
Pitcher of water (MAGGIE)
Drinking glass (MAGGIE)
Patient files (NURSE)
Medical chart (DOCTOR)

## SOUND EFFECTS

Phone ringing
Car engine (driving, then faster)
Doorbell
Answering machine beep

# NEW PLAYS

★ **HONOUR by Joanna Murray-Smith.** In a series of intense confrontations, a wife, husband, lover and daughter negotiate the forces of passion, history, responsibility and honour. "HONOUR makes for surprisingly interesting viewing. Tight, crackling dialogue (usually played out in punchy verbal duels) captures characters unable to deal with emotions … Murray-Smith effectively places her characters in situations that strip away pretense." –*Variety* "… the play's virtues are strong: a distinctive theatrical voice, passionate concerns … HONOUR might just capture a few honors of its own." –*Time Out Magazine* [1M, 3W] ISBN: 0-8222-1683-3

★ **MR. PETERS' CONNECTIONS by Arthur Miller.** Mr. Miller describes the protagonist as existing in a dream-like state when the mind is "freed to roam from real memories to conjectures, from trivialities to tragic insights, from terror of death to glorying in one's being alive." With this memory play, the Tony Award and Pulitzer Prize-winner reaffirms his stature as the world's foremost dramatist. "… a cross between Joycean stream-of-consciousness and Strindberg's dream plays, sweetened with a dose of William Saroyan's philosophical whimsy … CONNECTIONS is most intriguing …" –*The NY Times* [5M, 3W] ISBN: 0-8222-1687-6

★ **THE WAITING ROOM by Lisa Loomer.** Three women from different centuries meet in a doctor's waiting room in this dark comedy about the timeless quest for beauty – and its cost. "… THE WAITING ROOM … is a bold, risky melange of conflicting elements that is … terrifically moving … There's no resisting the fierce emotional pull of the play." –*The NY Times* "… one of the high points of this year's Off-Broadway season … THE WAITING ROOM is well worth a visit." –*Back Stage* [7M, 4W, flexible casting] ISBN: 0-8222-1594-2

★ **THE OLD SETTLER by John Henry Redwood.** A sweet-natured comedy about two church-going sisters in 1943 Harlem and the handsome young man who rents a room in their apartment. "For all of its decent sentiments, THE OLD SETTLER avoids sentimentality. It has the authenticity and lack of pretense of an Early American sampler." –*The NY Times* "We've had some fine plays Off-Broadway this season, and this is one of the best." –*The NY Post* [1M, 3W] ISBN: 0-8-222-1642-6

★ **LAST TRAIN TO NIBROC by Arlene Hutton.** In 1940 two young strangers share a seat on a train bound east only to find their paths will cross again. "All aboard. LAST TRAIN TO NIBROC is a sweetly told little chamber romance." –*Show Business* "… [a] gently charming little play, reminiscent of Thornton Wilder in its look at rustic Americans who are to be treasured for their simplicity and directness …" –*Associated Press* "The old formula of boy wins girl, boy loses girl, boy wins girl still works … [a] well-made play that perfectly captures a slice of small-town-life-gone-by." –*Back Stage* [1M, 1W] ISBN: 0-8222-1753-8

★ **OVER THE RIVER AND THROUGH THE WOODS by Joe DiPietro.** Nick sees both sets of his grandparents every Sunday for dinner. This is routine until he has to tell them that he's been offered a dream job in Seattle. The news doesn't sit so well. "A hilarious family comedy that is even funnier than his long running musical revue *I Love You, You're Perfect, Now Change*." –*Back Stage* "Loaded with laughs every step of the way." –*Star-Ledger* [3M, 3W] ISBN: 0-8222-1712-0

★ **SIDE MAN by Warren Leight.** 1999 Tony Award winner. This is the story of a broken family and the decline of jazz as popular entertainment. "… a tender, deeply personal memory play about the turmoil in the family of a jazz musician as his career crumbles at the dawn of the age of rock-and-roll …" –*The NY Times* "[SIDE MAN] is an elegy for two things – a lost world and a lost love. When the two notes sound together in harmony, it is moving and graceful …" –*The NY Daily News* "An atmospheric memory play…with crisp dialogue and clearly drawn characters … reflects the passing of an era with persuasive insight … The joy and despair of the musicians is skillfully illustrated." –*Variety* [5M, 3W] ISBN: 0-8222-1721-X

**DRAMATISTS PLAY SERVICE, INC.**
**440 Park Avenue South, New York, NY 10016  212-683-8960  Fax 212-213-1539**
postmaster@dramatists.com   www.dramatists.com

# NEW PLAYS

★ **CLOSER by Patrick Marber.** Winner of the 1998 Olivier Award for Best Play and the 1999 New York Drama Critics Circle Award for Best Foreign Play. Four lives intertwine over the course of four and a half years in this densely plotted, stinging look at modern love and betrayal. "CLOSER is a sad, savvy, often funny play that casts a steely, unblinking gaze at the world of relationships and lets you come to your own conclusions ... CLOSER does not merely hold your attention; it burrows into you." –*New York Magazine* "A powerful, darkly funny play about the cosmic collision between the sun of love and the comet of desire." –*Newsweek Magazine* [2M, 2W] ISBN: 0-8222-1722-8

★ **THE MOST FABULOUS STORY EVER TOLD by Paul Rudnick.** A stage manager, headset and prompt book at hand, brings the house lights to half, then dark, and cues the creation of the world. Throughout the play, she's in control of everything. In other words, she's either God, or she thinks she is. "Line by line, Mr. Rudnick may be the funniest writer for the stage in the United States today ... One-liners, epigrams, withering put-downs and flashing repartee: These are the candles that Mr. Rudnick lights instead of cursing the darkness ... a testament to the virtues of laughing ... and in laughter, there is something like the memory of Eden." –*The NY Times* "Funny it is ... consistently, rapaciously, deliriously ... easily the funniest play in town." –*Variety* [4M, 5W] ISBN: 0-8222-1720-1

★ **A DOLL'S HOUSE by Henrik Ibsen, adapted by Frank McGuinness.** Winner of the 1997 Tony Award for Best Revival. "New, raw, gut-twisting and gripping. Easily the hottest drama this season." –*USA Today* "Bold, brilliant and alive." –*The Wall Street Journal* "A thunderclap of an evening that takes your breath away." –*Time Magazine* [4M, 4W, 2 boys] ISBN: 0-8222-1636-1

★ **THE HERBAL BED by Peter Whelan.** The play is based on actual events which occurred in Stratford-upon-Avon in the summer of 1613, when William Shakespeare's elder daughter was publicly accused of having a sexual liaison with a married neighbor and family friend. "In his probing new play, THE HERBAL BED ... Peter Whelan muses about a sidelong event in the life of Shakespeare's family and creates a finely textured tapestry of love and lies in the early 17th-century Stratford." –*The NY Times* "It is a first rate drama with interesting moral issues of truth and expediency." –*The NY Post* [5M, 3W] ISBN: 0-8222-1675-2

★ **SNAKEBIT by David Marshall Grant.** A study of modern friendship when put to the test. "... a rather smart and absorbing evening of water-cooler theater, the intimate sort of Off-Broadway experience that has you picking apart the recognizable characters long after the curtain calls." – *The NY Times* "Off-Broadway keeps on presenting us with compelling reasons for going to the theater. The latest is SNAKEBIT, David Marshall Grant's smart new comic drama about being thirtysomething and losing one's way in life." –*The NY Daily News* [3M, 1W] ISBN: 0-8222-1724-4

★ **A QUESTION OF MERCY by David Rabe.** The Obie Award-winning playwright probes the sensitive and controversial issue of doctor-assisted suicide in the age of AIDS in this poignant drama. "There are many devastating ironies in Mr. Rabe's beautifully considered, piercingly clear-eyed work ..." –*The NY Times* "With unsettling candor and disturbing insight, the play arouses pity and understanding of a troubling subject ... Rabe's provocative tale is an affirmation of dignity that rings clear and true." –*Variety* [6M, 1W] ISBN: 0-8222-1643-4

★ **DIMLY PERCEIVED THREATS TO THE SYSTEM by Jon Klein.** Reality and fantasy overlap with hilarious results as this unforgettable family attempts to survive the nineties. "Here's a play whose point about fractured families goes to the heart, mind – and ears." –*The Washington Post* "... an end-of-the millennium comedy about a family on the verge of a nervous breakdown ... Trenchant and hilarious ..." –*The Baltimore Sun* [2M, 4W] ISBN: 0-8222-1677-9

**DRAMATISTS PLAY SERVICE, INC.**
440 Park Avenue South, New York, NY 10016  212-683-8960  Fax 212-213-1539
postmaster@dramatists.com  www.dramatists.com

# NEW PLAYS

★ **AS BEES IN HONEY DROWN by Douglas Carter Beane.** Winner of the John Gassner Playwriting Award. A hot young novelist finds the subject of his new screenplay in a New York socialite who leads him into the world of *Auntie Mame* and *Breakfast at Tiffany's*, before she takes him for a ride. "A delicious soufflé of a satire ... [an] extremely entertaining fable for an age that always chooses image over substance." *–The NY Times* "... A witty assessment of one of the most active and relentless industries in a consumer society ... the creation of 'hot' young things, which the media have learned to mass produce with efficiency and zeal." *–The NY Daily News* [3M, 3W, flexible casting] ISBN: 0-8222-1651-5

★ **STUPID KIDS by John C. Russell.** In rapid, highly stylized scenes, the story follows four high-school students as they make their way from first through eighth period and beyond, struggling with the fears, frustrations, and longings peculiar to youth. "In STUPID KIDS ... playwright John C. Russell gets the opera of adolescence to a T ... The stylized teenspeak of STUPID KIDS ... suggests that Mr. Russell may have hidden a tape recorder under a desk in study hall somewhere and then scoured the tapes for good quotations ... it is the kids' insular, ceaselessly churning world, a pre-adult world of Doritos and libidos, that the playwright seeks to lay bare." *–The NY Times* "STUPID KIDS [is] a sharp-edged ... whoosh of teen angst and conformity anguish. It is also very funny." *–NY Newsday* [2M, 2W] ISBN: 0-8222-1698-1

★ **COLLECTED STORIES by Donald Margulies.** From Obie Award-winner Donald Margulies comes a provocative analysis of a student-teacher relationship that turns sour when the protégé becomes a rival. "With his fine ear for detail, Margulies creates an authentic, insular world, and he gives equal weight to the opposing viewpoints of two formidable characters." *–The LA Times* "This is probably Margulies' best play to date ..." *–The NY Post* "... always fluid and lively, the play is thick with ideas, like a stock-pot of good stew." *–The Village Voice* [2W] ISBN: 0-8222-1640-X

★ **FREEDOMLAND by Amy Freed.** An overdue showdown between a son and his father sets off fireworks that illuminate the neurosis, rage and anxiety of one family – and of America at the turn of the millennium. "FREEDOMLAND's more obvious links are to *Buried Child* and *Bosoms and Neglect.* Freed, like Guare, is an inspired wordsmith with a gift for surreal touches in situations grounded in familiar and real territory." *–Curtain Up* [3M, 4W] ISBN: 0-8222-1719-8

★ **STOP KISS by Diana Son.** A poignant and funny play about the ways, both sudden and slow, that lives can change irrevocably. "There's so much that is vital and exciting about STOP KISS ... you want to embrace this young author and cheer her onto other works ... the writing on display here is funny and credible ... you also will be charmed by its heartfelt characters and up-to-the-minute humor." *–The NY Daily News* "... irresistibly exciting ... a sweet, sad, and enchantingly sincere play." *–The NY Times* [3M, 3W] ISBN: 0-8222-1731-7

★ **THREE DAYS OF RAIN by Richard Greenberg.** The sins of fathers and mothers make for a bittersweet elegy in this poignant and revealing drama. "... a work so perfectly judged it heralds the arrival of a major playwright ... Greenberg is extraordinary." *–The NY Daily News* "Greenberg's play is filled with graceful passages that are by turns melancholy, harrowing, and often, quite funny." *–Variety* [2M, 1W] ISBN: 0-8222-1676-0

★ **THE WEIR by Conor McPherson.** In a bar in rural Ireland, the local men swap spooky stories in an attempt to impress a young woman from Dublin who recently moved into a nearby "haunted" house. However, the tables are soon turned when she spins a yarn of her own. "You shed all sense of time at this beautiful and devious new play." *–The NY Times* "Sheer theatrical magic. I have rarely been so convinced that I have just seen a modern classic. Tremendous." *–The London Daily Telegraph* [4M, 1W] ISBN: 0-8222-1706-6

**DRAMATISTS PLAY SERVICE, INC.**
440 Park Avenue South, New York, NY 10016  212-683-8960  Fax 212-213-1539
postmaster@dramatists.com   www.dramatists.com